Narrative Constellations

Narrative Constellations

Exploring Lived Experience in Education

Susanne Garvis
University of Gothenburg, Sweden

SENSE PUBLISHERS
ROTTERDAM/BOSTON/TAIPEI

A C.I.P. record for this book is available from the Library of Congress.

ISBN: 978-94-6300-149-6 (paperback)
ISBN: 978-94-6300-150-2 (hardback)
ISBN: 978-94-6300-151-9 (e-book)

Published by: Sense Publishers,
P.O. Box 21858,
3001 AW Rotterdam,
The Netherlands
https://www.sensepublishers.com/

Printed on acid-free paper

All Rights Reserved © 2015 Sense Publishers

No part of this work may be reproduced, stored in a retrieval system, or transmitted in any form or by any means, electronic, mechanical, photocopying, microfilming, recording or otherwise, without written permission from the Publisher, with the exception of any material supplied specifically for the purpose of being entered and executed on a computer system, for exclusive use by the purchaser of the work.

TABLES OF CONTENTS

Preface	vii
Chapter 1: What Is the Narrative Genre?	1
Introduction	1
Constructing and Co-Constructing Lived Experience	1
Terminology	2
Narrative Inquiry	3
Interactions	4
Researcher's Role	5
Narrative Analysis	6
Validity	7
Conclusion	7
Chapter 2: What Are Constellation Narratives?	11
Introduction	11
Story Constellations	12
Collecting Data for the Story Constellation	13
The Professional Knowledge Landscape	16
Constructing and (Re)Presenting the Research Text	16
Trustworthiness	20
Reflexivity and Subjectivity	22
Limitations	23
Conclusion	23
Chapter 3: At This School Arts Education Is Travelling on a Rocky Road	29
Introduction	29
Introducing Tabitha's One Teacher Rural School	29
Teacher Story	32
School Story	37
Curriculum Story	40
Community Story	42
Reform Story	43

TABLE OF CONTENTS

Chapter 4: At This School Arts Education Is Part of the Holistic Development of All Girls ... 47

Introduction ... 47
Introducing the Maxwell Girls Schools ... 47
Teacher Story ... 48
Principal Story ... 54
School Story ... 57
Community Story ... 61
Reform Story ... 62

Chapter 5: Assessment Is a Holistic Judgement: Do I Want This Pre-Service Teacher Teaching My Children? ... 67

Introduction ... 67
Introducing the Kindergarten ... 67
Supervising Teacher Story ... 68
Duelling Roles Exist ... 71
Pre-Service Teacher Story ... 73
Communication Is Important ... 74
University Teacher Story ... 76

Chapter 6: The Future and Narrative Constellations ... 83

Introduction ... 83
What Have We Learnt from Narrative Constellations? ... 83
What about the Future? ... 86
Conclusion ... 88

PREFACE

Narrative research in contemporary times can free social scientists from the rhetorical forms (Emihovich, 1995) that alienate children and families from their own traditions. Through the use of narrative we are able to recognise the power of subjectivity in allowing open dialogue and co-construction of meaning. Becoming comfortable with narrative research also means accepting ideas that the world has no fixed rules for assigning behaviour (Emihovich, 1995). This means that open dialogue is required to build consensus around shared meaning and to ensure the inclusion of multiple voices. Thus as Bruner (1986, p. 144) notes, "narrative structures are not only structures of meaning but structures of power as well". It is for this reason that it is important to explore narratives.

Over time I have also come to realise the importance of sharing ideas about methodology and methods with the wider research community. Rather than continue to work in isolated pockets, it is important for us to share and discuss our research ideas and processes. In this book I have shared the narrative genre with a specific focus on story constellations. I believe that narratives are important for understanding the lived experiences of humans. Together we can explore the complexity of life and experience rather than having a 'technocratic' understanding of the world. The narrative genre provides the opportunity

The initial ideas about this book have come from my supervision of PhD and Master research students who are always looking for a good text about narrative approaches and story constellations. Realising that the students needed reading material, my thoughts were focused on their needs and how to best support their learning and understanding.

The book begins with a theoretical overview of narrative genre before focusing on narrative constellations. Three constellations are then shared with the reader. The final chapter provides ideas about the future of narrative constellation in research and the impact constellations can have to future policy and practice. It is hoped that the reader develops a better understanding of narrative ways and begins to see the potential of narrative constellations in the research genre.

PREFACE

REFERENCES

Bruner, J. S. (1986). *Actual minds, possible worlds.* Cambridge, MA: Harvard University Press.

Emilhovich, C. (1995). Distancing passion: Narratives in social science. In J. A. Hatch & R. Wisniewski (Eds.), *Life histories and narrative* (pp. 37–48). London: Falmer Press.

CHAPTER 1

WHAT IS THE NARRATIVE GENRE?

INTRODUCTION

Narrative has had a rich intellectual tradition. Many disciplines believe that human experience is a narrative phenomena that is best understood through story. This includes researchers in the disciplines of anthropology, linguistics, literary theory, philosophy, pscyhology, theology, women's studies, organizational theory, psychotherapy, geography, history, law and medicine (Craig, 2007). Narrative tradition can be traced back to Aristotle (Bruner, 2002) with the importance of lived experience. Some researchers suggest narratives goes back further to when early humans began grunting and creating senses of their experiences around camp fires (LeGuin, 1989).

This chapter will explore the concept of lived experience and the relationship to the narrative genre. It will explore the pillars of narrative and provide the reader with a better understanding of lived experience as a personal research method.

CONSTRUCTING AND CO-CONSTRUCTING LIVED EXPERIENCE

Bruner (1986) describes narratives as forms of oral discourse that characterise and facilitate culturally determined ways of communicating lived or imagined events to others. As such, narratives are the way in which individuals represent and make sense of past experience, evaluate experiences in the present and plan and anticipate future experiences. The intersection is also based on the scientific potential of exploring children's narratives to show relationships between human experience and narrative. Narrative research is often inspired by a view of human experience that is based on John's Dewey's pragmatic philosophy (Clandinin, 2006). Children's experiences in their everyday life are represented in the form of narratives and stories (Riessman, 1993). Starting from this point of view, narratives allow researchers insights in the experience of a child or adult's world. In a developmental sense, it also represents the current state of the child's development by showing representation of the child level of understanding. The child is considered competent and capable in displaying how they come

1

CHAPTER 1

to know and understand the world around them. Children choose how they would like to communicate this meaning to adults.

The process of narration is also a culture-specific process that can represent a potential framework for enhancing contextualist theories of development (Bruner, 1990). Narrative can bridge cultural modes of thinking and the ways in which children come to reasons and behave in culture-specific ways. In this way, children's thinking reflects the modes of thinking of those who collectively make up a particular cultural group in which the children collaborates. Contemporary issues of place become important in analysis. The concept of place becomes a key features in how children interact and communicate with each other.

Narrative is considered a 'universal mode of thought' and a 'form of thinking' (Bruner, 1986; Nelson, 2006). According to Haakarainen et al. (2013, p. 215), "from the cultural-historical perspective, a narrative could be defined as a psychological tool formalising and unifying human thought and knowledge into thematic units- units of thought". Accordingly, narrative is the smallest cell of human thinking, providing insight into the child's experiences. As Vygotsky described (1978, p. 126), "thought undergoes many changes as it turns into speech. It does not merely find expression in speech; it finds reality and form"

Bruner (1986) describes narratives as forms of oral discourse that characterise and facilitate culturally determined ways of communicating lived or imagined events to others. As such, narratives are the way in which individuals represent and make sense of past experience, evaluate experiences in the present and plan and anticipate future experiences.

Narrative research in contemporary times can also free social scientists from the rhetorical forms (Emihovich, 1995) that alienate children and families from their own traditions. Through the use of narrative we are able to recognise the power of subjectivity in allowing open dialogue and co-construction of meaning. Becoming comfortable with narrative research also means accepting ideas that the world has no fixed rules for assigning behaviour (Emihovich, 1995). This means that open dialogue is required to build consensus around shared meaning and to ensure the inclusion of multiple voices. Thus as Bruner (1986, p. 144) notes, "narrative structures are not only structures of meaning but structures of power as well".

TERMINOLOGY

There is a distinction between *Narrative,* meaning both a story and its telling; the process of constructing story. *Narrative methodology* will refer

WHAT IS THE NARRATIVE GENRE?

to research in the scientific landscape where narrative is used in ways that differ (for example as the products of anthropology and case studies, and as methods like in ethnography and in interviews). *Narrative analysis* will mean an approach where the researcher narrates based on data. Since analysis always will be the researchers construct, this will also include *analysis of narrative*, which is also a certain approach, where the researcher analyse stories (Polkinghorne, 1995). *Narrative inquiry* will here refer to a method of investigation into a problem, following pragmatism, inspired by John Dewey. Following this tradition, narrative inquiry will also mean a way of knowing by telling and reflecting. *Narrative inquiry* is a way of understanding experience. It is collaboration between researchers and participants, over time in a place or series of places, and in social interaction with milieus (Clandinin & Connelly, 2000, p. 20). In this particular focus on narrative constellations, narrative inquiry is the focus.

NARRATIVE INQUIRY

The collective case studies are informed by the narrative approach. As an epistemological approach, narrative inquiry seeks to understand human subjective experience by making people's stories a central focus of research (Clandinin, 2006, 2007; Clandinin & Connelly, 2000; Connelly & Clandinin, 1990). Clandinin and Connelly have conceptualised narrative inquiry as:

> a way of understanding experience. It is a collaboration between researcher and participants, over time, in a place or series of places, and in social interaction with milieus. An inquirer enters this matrix … in the midst of living and telling, reliving and retelling, the stories of the experiences that make up people's lives, both individual and social. Simply stated, … narrative inquiry is stories lived and told. (2000, p. 20)

It is through the processes of telling and listening to stories that people narratively construct, and continually re-construct, who they are (Bruner, 2002; Clandinin & Connelly, 2000; Connelly & Clandinin, 1990; Kenyon & Randall, 1997; Mishler, 2004; Søreide, 2006; Watson, 2006; Wortham, 2000). Additionally, narrative inquirers argue that, given that storied experience is so essential to identity and self (McAdams et al., 2006, p. xi), human experience is best understood through narrative (Clandinin & Connelly, 2000, p. 20).

The use of narrative inquiry across disciplines stems from the realisation that traditional empirical research methods "cannot sufficiently address

3

CHAPTER 1

issues such as complexity, multiplicity of perspective and human centredness" (Webster & Mertova, 2007, p. 31). These issues can be more adequately addressed through narrative inquiry (Webster & Mertova, 2007). Narrative inquiry therefore is first and foremost a way of thinking about experience (Connelly & Clandinin, 2006). Since values and beliefs are based on experience, a narrative approach is ideally suited to inform this study.

In the field, researcher-participant relationships underpin much of what narrative inquirers do (Clandinin & Connelly, 2000), because entering the field to investigate the lived experience of participants means entering their social world and being in it with them (Ezzy, 2002). Narrative inquirers are therefore said to live and work alongside participants in their stories (Clandinin & Connelly, 2000). Accordingly, it is this living and working alongside that makes narrative inquiry "the most compelling and appropriate way to study human interaction" (Clandinin & Connelly, 2000, as cited in Pinnegar & Daynes, 2007, p. 6).

The primary research products of a narrative inquiry are constructed, or co-constructed, accounts that re-present people's personal and professional experiences (Clandinin & Connelly, 2000). Reading these accounts offers an opportunity for others to develop insights into, or come to understand, the ways in which particular individuals have been affected by the happenings in their lives (Dunn, 2003; Kelchtermans, 1993; Trzebiński, 2005).

INTERACTIONS

Narrative research often relies on verbal language through interaction. Children will use a range of narrative means to share, express and organize their experiences (Ahn & Filipenko, 2007; Engel, 2006; Puroila, Estola, & Sryala, 2012). This type of multimodal expression from children requires sensitive listening from the adult's side. The role of the adult is to analyse and explore the narrative constructions of the child.

One theory useful for adults to understand is interaction theory. Interaction theory is described as a larger enactive or phenomenological approach to social cognition (Gallagher, 2012). Interaction theory (Gallagher, 2013, p. 5) relies "on developmental studies that demonstrate that our encounters with others are best characterized in terms of embodied interactions rather than the kind of mind reading defended by simulation theory or other theory-of-mind approaches". While there is much potential for the intersection of narrative perspectives with developmental perspectives, there is still a lack of empirical base research to support this combination (Bruner, 2004; Habermas

4

& Bluck, 2000; Mulvaney, 2011). The narrative perspective has potentially broad implications for developmental theories but requires additional types of research to fully exploit its potential.

RESEARCHER'S ROLE

Part of the narrative genre is also exploring the role of the researcher. Often in quantitative research the role of the researcher is not important to the research. In narratives studies, the role of the researcher is important for all elements of the study as the researchers shapes and interprets all areas.

Part of the researcher's role also includes their credibility to the participants they are involved with. As a teacher of seven years experience who has worked in four different schools, I am viewed as credible by the teaching profession when researching education. I do not encounter problems of accessing the setting, understanding the language and culture of the respondents and deciding on how to present oneself (Fontana & Frey, 2000). I do however need to gain the participants' trust. As Clandinin and Connelly (2000, p. 110) suggest, "the way an interviewer acts, questions and responds in an interview shapes the relationship and therefore the ways participants respond and give accounts of their experiences". I draw on personal experiences of teaching to put the participants at ease and provide an encouraging environment. By illustrating my experience and understanding of the phenomenon from a 'teaching perspective', I was able to build respect and trust with the participant rather than provide a set of examples of what I was looking for.

Researcher-participant relationships underpin much of what narrative inquirers do (Clandinin & Connelly, 2000). Subsequently, the quality of the relationship between the researcher and the participants can determine both the quality and the quantity of the data generated (Kelchtermans, 1999). Participants who trust the researcher and feel safe in the relationship are more inclined to share their stories (Kelchtermans, 1999). The quality of the relationships that are built, and the stories that are shared, tend to reflect the depth of the personal, emotional impact on researchers who choose to study social processes (Chambliss & Schutt, 2003, p. 174).

Establishing good relationships with participants is essential to the conduct of the best qualitative research, because it is not possible for researchers to understand people by being distant from them (Ezzy, 2002). Narrative inquirers "recognize and embrace the interactive quality of the researcher-researched relationship" (Pinnegar & Daynes, 2007, p. 7). This means

CHAPTER 1

that throughout all stages of the research project, the researcher must be continually focused on relationships and the importance of relationality. It is through building relationships that participants can trust and start to share their real stories of lived experience.

NARRATIVE ANALYSIS

Narrative analysis is used within narrative inquiry. Narrative analysis is appropriate because it "allows for systematic study of personal experience and meaning" (Riessman, 1993, p. 70). Narrative researchers construct stories from descriptive data relating to the phenomena under study (p. 15). According to Polkinghorne (1995, p. 15), to begin this process, the researcher asks:

> Questions such as "How did this happen?" or "Why did this come about?" and searches for pieces of information that contribute to the construction of a story that provides an explanatory answer to the questions.

My initial search is for "chunks of interview text about particular themes," that are meaningful and relevant to the study and figure "importantly and repeatedly" (Riessman, 1993, p. 67). I try and work these themes over and over again to find these 'meaningful chunks'. It soon becomes apparent that a "theme is worked over, again and again" (Riessman, 1993, p. 67) in each of the interviews. Initially my analysis is inductive (Janesick, 2000, p. 389). It is concerned with locating thematic elements and the "narrative threads" or "story lines" interwoven and interconnected throughout the data sets (Clandinin & Connelly, 2000, pp. 131–133).

Analysis becomes an "increasingly complex" task, involving reading, and "relentlessly rereading," the field texts (interview transcripts and observational field notes) of each participant, in order to "narratively code" the data (Clandinin & Connelly, 2000, p. 131). I begin to see meaning in the field text. However, Clandinin and Connelly argue that no matter how compelling our narrative inquiry field texts are, we need to "fight against our desire to let [them] speak for themselves" (2000, p. 130; see also Gough, 2003, p. 30). Rather, Clandinin and Connelly (2000, p. 130) advise that we must go further, and reconstruct our field texts (e.g., field notes and interview transcripts) as research texts (scholarly accounts) because "our inquiry task is to discover and construct meaning". Through an ongoing process of construction and reconstruction of meaning, field texts are able to be turned into publishable research texts (Clandinin & Connelly, 1994).

The next stage of analysis is broadening, burrowing, and restorying' (Connelly & Clandinin, 1990) interpretive devices used in order to create the form of the story constellation. Each of the interpretive devices allows the triangulation and transformation of field texts into research texts (Garvis, 2010).

Broadening can be described as the small picture. In this, the general context of where the relationships and partnerships take place is set up. Broadening helps to explain the socio political, physical and structural (Craig, 2007). Burrowing (Connelly & Clandinin, 1990) is going deeper into the 'big picture'. This involves listening closely to how individuals string their life experiences together to make personal sense of them (Craig, 2007). Finally, restorying captures the transitions in how the story is told and retold, the competing commitments underlying how people make sense of the shared interaction (Garvis, 2010).

VALIDITY

Validity in narrative research refers to the "believability of a statement or knowledge claim" (Polkinghorne, 2007, p. 474). Thus, readers will judge the validity of our work as researchers; they are the people who must be convinced that a knowledge claim is justified. Differences emerge however based on people's view points. It is for this reason traditional understandings of validity may not represent the postmodern world. Alternative notions of validity can be used such as trustworthiness (Lincoln & Guba, 1985), "verisimilitude" (Ellis & Bochner, 2000, p. 751), "truthlike observations" (Barone & Eisner, 1997, p. 74) and "crystallisation" (Richardson, 2000, p. 934). For example, Richardson's (2000) notion of "crystallization- deconstructs the traditional idea of 'validity'" by recognising that there are more than three sides (reliability, validity and generalisability) from which to view the world. Polkinghorne (2007) further suggests that in narrative research readers are asked "to make judgements on whether or not the evidence and argument convinces them at the level of plausibility, credibleness, or trustworthiness of the claim" (p. 477). Validity therefore relates to personal meaning drawn from the narrative stories, not to a measurable truth.

CONCLUSION

Narrative inquiry offers many possibilities for researchers. This chapter has shown understanding of narrative inquiry. The importance of narrative as a research method becomes known. The next chapter focuses on constellation

CHAPTER 1

narratives. It will explore the details of data collection, analysis and creation of the research text. It will attempt to answer the' how questions' of constellation narratives. Chapter three, four and five provides examples of the constellation narrative approach. As you read the constellations, you will notice the different context as well as the different voices within each of the constellations. In chapter three there is one voice, in chapter four there are two voices and in chapter five there are three voices in a practice triad. The final chapter explores the possibilities of narrative constellations in research.

REFERENCES

Ahn, J., & Filipenko, M. (2007). Narrative, imaginary play, art, and self: Intersecting worlds. *Early Childhood Education Journal, 34*, 279–289.

Barone, T., & Eisner, E. W. (1997). Arts-based educational research. In R. M. Jaeger (Ed.), *Complementary methods for research in education* (2nd ed.). Washington, DC: AERA.

Bruner, J. (1986). *Actual minds, possible worlds.* Cambridge, MA: Harvard University Press.

Bruner, J. (2002). *Making stories: Law, literature, life.* New York, NY: Farrar, Strauss & Girony.

Bruner, J. (2004). Life as narrative. *Social Research, 71*, 691–710.

Chambliss, D. F., & Schutt, R. K. (2003). *Making sense of the social world: Methods of investigation.* Thousand Oaks, CA: Sage.

Clandinin, D. J. (2006). Narrative inquiry: A methodology for studying lived experience. *Research studies in music education, 27*, 45–55.

Clandinin, D. J. (Ed.). (2007). *Handbook of narrative inquiry.* London, UK: Sage.

Clandinin, D. J., & Connelly, F. M. (2000). *Narrative inquiry.* San Francisco, CA: Jossey-Bass.

Connelly, F. M., & Clandinin, D. J. (1990). Stories of experience and narrative inquiry, *Educational Researcher, 19*(5), 2–14.

Connelly, F. M., & Clandinin, D. J. (2006). Narrative inquiry. In J. L. Green, G. Camilli, & P. B. Elmore (Eds.), *Handbook of complementary methods in education research* (3rd ed., pp. 477–487). Mahwah, NJ: Lawrence Erlbaum.

Dunn, D. S. (2003). Teach me about your life: Narrative approaches to lives, meaning, and transitions. *Journal of Social and Clinical Psychology, 22*(5), 604–606.

Ellis, C., & Bochner, A. (2000). Autoethnography, personal narrative, reflexivity: Researcher as subject. In N. Denzin & Y. Lincoln (Eds.), *The handbook of qualitative research* (2nd ed.) (pp. 733–768). Newbury Park, CA: Sage.

Emilhovich, C. (1995). Distancing passion: Narratives in social science. In J. A. Hatch & R. Wisniewski (Eds), *Life histories and narrative* (pp. 37–48). London, UK: Falmer Press.

Engel, S. (2006). Narrative analysis of children's experience. In S. Greene & D. Hogan (Eds.), *Researching children's experience: Approaches and methods* (pp. 199–216). London, UK: Sage.

Ezzy, D. (2002). *Qualitative analysis: Practice and innovation.* Crows Nest, NSW, Australia: Allen & Unwin.

8

Fontana, A., & Frey, J. H. (2000). The interview: From structured questions to negotiated text. In N. K. Denzin & Y. S. Lincoln (Eds.) *Handbook of qualitative research*. Thousand Oaks, CA: Sage.

Gallagher, S. (2013). An education in narratives. *Educational Philosophy and Theory*. doi: http://dx.doi.org/10.1080/00131857.2013.779213

Gallagher, S. (2012). In defense of phenomenological approaches to social cognition: Interacting with the critics. *Review of Philosophy and Psychology*, *3*, 187–212.

Habermas, T., & Bluck, S. (2000). Getting a life: The emergence of the life story in adolescence. *Psychological Bulletin*, *126*, 748–769.

Hakkarainen, P., Brėdikytė, M., Jakkula, K., & Munter, H. (2013). Adult play guidance and children's play development in a narrative play-world, *European Early Childhood Education Research Journal*, *21*(2), 213–225.

Janesick, V. (2000). The choreography of qualitative research design: Minuets, improvisations, and crystallization. In N. K. Denzin & Y. S. Lincoln (Eds.), *Handbook of qualitative research* (2nd ed., pp. 379–400). Thousand Oaks, CA: Sage.

Kelchtermans, G. (1999). *Narrative-biographical research on teachers' professional development: Exemplifying a methodological research procedure*. Presented at Annual Meeting of the American Educational Research Association, New York, NY.

Kelchtermans, G. (1993). Teachers and their career story: A biographical perspective on professional development. In C. Day, J. Calderhead, & P. Denicolo (Eds.), *Research on teacher thinking: Towards understanding professional development* (pp. 198–220). London, UK: Falmer Press.

Kenyon, G., & Randall, W. (1997) *Restorying our lives: Personal growth through autobiographical reflection*. Westport, CT: Praeger.

Lincoln, Y. S., & Guba, E. G. (1985). *Naturalistic inquiry*. Beverly Hills, CA: Sage.

McAdams, D. P., Bauer, J. J., Sakaeda, A. R., Anyidoho, N. A., Machado, M. A., Magrino-Failla, K., White, K. W., & Pals, J. L. (2006). Continuity and change in the life story: A longitudinal study of autobiographical memories in emerging adulthood. *Journal of Personality*, *74*(5), 1371–1400.

Mishler, E. G. (2004). Historians of the self: Restorying lives, revising identities. *Research in Human Development*, *1*(1 & 2), 101–121.

Mulvaney, M. K. (2011) Narrative processes across childhood. *Early Child Development and Care*, *181*(9), 1153–1161.

Nelson, K. (2007). *Narratives from the crib: With a new foreword by Emily Oster, the child in the crib*. USA: Harvard University Press.

Pinnegar, S., & Daynes, J. G. (2007). Locating narrative inquiry historically: Thematics in the turn to narrative. In D. J. Clandinin (Ed.), *Handbook of narrative inquiry: Mapping a methodology* (pp. 3–34). London: Sage. Retrieved February 20, 2007, from http://www.Sagepub.com/upm-data/13548_ Chapter1.pdf

Polkinghorne, D. (2007). Validity issues in narrative research. *Qualitative Inquiry*, *13*(4), 471–486.

Polkinghorne, D. (1995). Narrative configuration in qualitative analysis. In J. A. Hatch & R. Wisniewski (Eds.), *Life history and narrative* (pp. 5–21). London, UK: The Falmer Press.

Puroila, A.-M., Estola, E., & Syrjälä, L. (2012). Does Santa exist? Children's everyday narratives as dynamic meeting places in a day care centre context. *Early Child Development and Care*, *182*(2), 191–206.

CHAPTER 1

Richardson, L. (2000). Writing: A method of inquiry. In N. K. Denzin & Y. S. Lincoln (Eds.), *Handbook of qualitative research* (2nd ed., pp. 923–943). Thousand Oaks, CA: Sage.

Riessman, C. K. (1993). *Narrative analysis*. Newbury Park, CA: Sage.

Søreide, G. E. (2006). Narrative construction of teacher identity: Positioning and negotiation. *Teachers and Teaching: Theory and Practice, 12*(5), 527–547.

Trzebiński, J. (2005). Narratives and understanding other people. *Research in Drama Education, 10*(1), 15–25.

Vygotsky, L. (1978). *Mind in society: The development of higher psychological processes*. Cambridge, MA: Harvard University Press.

Watson, C. (2006). Narratives of practice and the construction of identity in teaching. *Teachers and Teaching: Theory and Practice, 12*(5), 509–526.

Webster, L., & Mertova, P. (2007). *Using narrative inquiry as a research method*. New York, NY: Routledge.

Wortham, S. (2000). Interactional positioning and narrative self-construction. *Narrative Inquiry, 10*(1), 157–184.

CHAPTER 2

WHAT ARE CONSTELLATION NARRATIVES?

INTRODUCTION

Constellation narratives are part of the narrative genre. I consider that constellation narratives are located in the interpretivist paradigm. My approach to research, then, is one in which knowledge is considered to be a subjective "human construction" (Hatch, 2002, p. 13). As an interpretivist researcher, I understand that "knowledge is socially constructed" (Denzin & Lincoln, 2000, p. 8).

An interpretivist approach can facilitate insights into emotions, meaning and reasons for actions. As Schwandt (1994, p. 118) suggests, "to understand the world of meaning, one must interpret it". An interpetivist position therefore suggests that:

> [m]eaning – and hence, reality – is constructed through the social interaction of people within a social setting. Meanings change in the course of interaction because the participants hold different perceptions; thus, reality is flexible and based on interpretations, rather than fixed. (Bennett & LeCompte, 1990, p. 32)

Interpretivists believe that reality is not objectively determined, but is socially constructed (Husserl, 1965). As an interpretivist, I recognise that multiple realities exist (Bogdan & Biklen, 1998; Bruner, 1986; Hatch, 2002; Polkinghorne, 1988), and I understand that these realities are "inherently unique because they are constructed by individuals who experience the world from their own vantage points" (Hatch, 2002, p. 15). This view is always filtered through the lens of the social world to which the individual belongs (Bruner, 1986; Clandinin & Connelly, 1994). In narrative constellation study, I am seeking an understanding, through a search for meaning (Barone, 2001).

This chapter will provide a detailed understanding of constellation narratives. It will describe the 'how to' of the research process and discuss important considerations including the research text and leaving the research field.

11

CHAPTER 2

STORY CONSTELLATIONS

Through living and telling, and re-living and re-telling, beginning teachers' stories of experience and their personal practical knowledge can be expressed. Indeed, narratives serve as a method of interpretation and reinterpretation of experience (Carter, 1993; Huber & Whelan, 2001). In this study, I have chosen a story constellation approach to help interpret and reinterpret the experience of beginning teachers with the data gained from the case studies.

In a story constellation, an individuals' narratives of experience relate to each another (Garvis, 2010). Their narratives of experience are always shifting, "each with a unique spiralling pattern, necessarily involving many plotlines, which, in turn, bring multiple meanings to bear on teachers' knowledge as shaped in their reforming school contexts" (Craig, 2007, p. 4). Through this approach, "a constellation of factors ... including the moralities and mores of teachers" (Schwab, 1970, pp. 8–10), is brought to the surface for discussion and analysis. Through this approach, key ideas become known for discussion and analysis (Garvis, 2010).

The story constellation approach attempts to locate teachers' knowledge in the multiple contexts within which it is created. According to Craig (2007, p. 6):

> Constellations allow for school life to be characterized without the flattening or dismissing of teachers' and principals' knowledge and their relationships and interactions amid the flow of events in the educational enterprise ... [where] ... the constraints of both formalist and reductionist investigations are avoided.

The story constellations approach opens out in a three-dimensional space (Clandinin & Connelly, 2000), and is comprised of: the temporal (past, present, and future), the personal and social (interaction), and the contextual (situation and place). The stories that people tell are influenced by each of these dimensions. Researchers must therefore pay particular attention to these dimensions in their research and the way they present research texts.

Clandinin and Connelly (1996) suggest many plotlines can be presented as paired narratives. Among these narratives, stories of teachers/teacher stories and stories of school/school stories stood out (Clandinin & Connelly, 1996). Teacher stories are stories told by teachers, whereas stories of teachers (the partner story) are stories told about teachers. Similarly, stories of school are stories given to schools, whereas school stories are stories told by schools. In the story constellation approach, Craig (2001) introduces two other sets of stories to the matrix: stories of community/community stories and stories of

12

WHAT ARE CONSTELLATION NARRATIVES?

reform/reform stories. Accordingly, stories of community are the stories told about communities, whereas community stories are stories that communities tell (Craig, 2007). Stories of reform are stories told about school reform, whereas reform stories are stories educators tell about the human experience of how reform stories become lived in school contexts (Craig, 2007). By providing these extra paired stories to the matrix, additional perspectives are offered on the complex influences within the school. When the stories are juxtaposed with one another, they create story constellations that capture unique combinations of narratives lived and told within school landscapes (Craig, 2007).

The strengths of the story constellations approach are its sensitivity to both teachers' developing knowledge and schools' shifting contexts and the way the approach enables researchers to follow where an unfolding story may lead (Craig, 2007). Moreover, it allows teachers' practical experiences, rather than researchers' theoretical perspectives, to take the lead in the 'methodological dance' (Janesick, 1994).

This approach however does have drawbacks. The most obvious is the lack of generalizability to other teachers and other school contexts – although the possibility of transferability exists (Lincoln & Guba, 1985). While Stake (1995, p. 7) acknowledges "case study seems a poor basis for generalization", he acknowledges that from a collection of case studies we may make '*petite generalizations*'. In this study, I shall make several '*petite generalizations*' that are possible with collective case studies.

Craig (2007, p. 203) suggests that "the ultimate danger (some might say promise) of story constellations as a form of narrative inquiry lies in the fact that when it is done well, people are likely to be disturbed by it and the disequilibrium that ensues may lead to change – though not always in ways that can be predicted" (Lincoln, 2003 cited in Craig, 2007, p. 14). In my narrative constellation studies, I endeavour to create story constellations that provide a comprehensive account of people's beliefs, values and experiences. I have used narrative constellations in early childhood, primary school and secondary school to highlight educational spaces.

COLLECTING DATA FOR THE STORY CONSTELLATION

Interviews

I considered interviews to be effective means for researchers to understand the meaning that participants make of any experience, as "the very process of putting experience into language is a meaning-making process" (Vygotsky,

CHAPTER 2

as cited in Seidman, 1991, p. 12). Interviews are an established method of gathering data in the social sciences (Fontana & Frey, 1998, 2000; Gubrium & Holstein, 2002). Interviews involve individual, face-to-face verbal interchanges (Fontana & Frey, 2000).

Often multiple semi-structured interviews are used in story constellations. By having two semi-structured interviews, I want to "establish a substantial relationship with participants over time" (Seidman, 1991, p. 15). The advantage inherent in this relationship is that interviewees come to better understand the value that researchers place on their participants' "experiences and points of view" (Kirkevold & Bergland, 2007, p. 73). This relational understanding between researcher and participants is congruent with the philosophies at the heart of narrative inquiry (Clandinin & Connelly, 2000), and acknowledged my need to find an appropriate and sympathetic means of generating data for the purpose of this study.

In my story constellations I adapt the three interview series (Seidman, 1991). Seidman (1991) describes this process as a series of three (90-minute) interviews conducted with individual interviewees. The design of each interview is based on the belief that "people's behaviour becomes meaningful and understandable when placed in the context of their lives and the lives of those around them" (Seidman, 1991, p. 10).

Because of time factors and the diverse geographical locations of the participants, I have sometimes turned the three interviews series into two interviews. The first interview is often designed around the personal experiences, values and beliefs of the participant. It is designed to elicit contextual data from participants by taking a life history interview approach (Seidman, 1991) of their levied experience. The interview is conducted at the educational context at a time convenient to the participant. The second and third interview are designed to investigate the professional beliefs, values and experience. During these interviews, I want participants to "reflect on the on the meaning their experience holds for them" (Seidman, 1991, p. 11). Seidman (1991, p. 14) suggests follow up interviews should be spaced "from three days to a week apart". Subsequently, I often have to plan well in advance the interview series.

Sometimes I also engage in artefact elicitation to help prompt discussion within the interview. Participants are invited to bring an artefact from their professional engagement. No boundaries are imposed on the choice of artefacts. This process of artefact elicitation enables participants to "externalise their knowledge that would otherwise remain inaccessible" (Teeavarunyou & Sato, 2001, p. 1). Through this process, participants reflect

WHAT ARE CONSTELLATION NARRATIVES?

on their own experiences. Artefact elicitation therefore provides a means of eliciting knowledge and attitudes that may have remained hidden during the interview process (Barrett & Smigel, 2003).

Conducting the Interview

After finalising the interview process, appointments are made with each participant. By allowing the participants to be in their natural context, it allows them to express themselves more fully (Lawrence-Lightfoot & Davis, 1997). Adopting Kvale's (1996, p. 4) metaphor of a "traveller" on a journey gathering stories, I was able to collect stories from educational contexts.

Believing that "interviews are social interactions" (Mason, 1998, p. 40), I adopt a conversational style throughout the interviews where I share my stories, as well as actively listen to the participant. This approach generates "long and uninterrupted narratives" (Holstein & Gubrium, 2003, as cited in Kirkevold & Bergland, 2007, p. 68), although this outcome is reliant upon the narrative competence of the participants, and the restraint of the interviewer, to at least some degree. The conversational nature of the interviews actively encouraged participants to elaborate further on their experiences (Kirkevold & Bergland, 2007).

Recording Interviews and Field Notes

I arrive early at each educational context to ensure I am prepared. During this time, I also take field notes on the physical description of the educational context to help me remember the school context. The field notes help me develop a greater understanding of the context.

I always digitally record interviews. All of the participants I have interviewed have never had a reservation about being digitally recorded. I believe part of this is because interviews questions are shown in advance.

The digital recorder is placed on the table so that it can pick up voices clearly, yet be unobtrusive to the interview. The presence of these recording tools during the interviews is "routinely ignored" by participants (Chambliss & Schutt, 2003, p. 180). I also take written notes during the interviews, observing the movements and gestures of the participants as they communicate what is being said.

At the end of an interview, I have found that participants regularly add to interview conversation as they walk out of their office, school or classroom (Chambliss & Schutt, 2003, p. 180). Afterwards, I would record as much as I could recall of these continuances as field notes.

CHAPTER 2

After the Interview

The recorded interviews are transcribed in their entirety, word for word as spoken, that is, "with no respect for the rules of written language" (Rosenthal, 1993, p. 71). The transcriptions are checked against the audio recording for accuracy, "establishing dependability and confirmability" (Easton et al., 2000, p. 707). Listening to the interview conversations during the processes of accuracy checking is the next cognitive step in my analysis (Kvale, 1996, p. 16).

I often send the transcripts to the participant for member checking. This process results in a few minor corrections to the transcript from interviewees. I also allow participants to choose a pseudonym for themselves and their educational context. The participants appear to thoroughly enjoy this process of creating a fictional identity. As one principal once commented, "this is all really exciting to choose another identity. I can be anyone I want" (Garvis, 2010).

THE PROFESSIONAL KNOWLEDGE LANDSCAPE

By narratively constructing constellations, it is possible "to elaborate on the professional knowledge landscape conceptualisation" (Craig, 2003, p. 176). In narrative constellation studies, each educational context has a different backdrop, with different school procedures, timetable and philosophy. Each educational context also approaches concepts of teaching and learning in different ways highlighting differences created by lived experiences. These combinations of exploring a range of educational contexts bring new perspectives about educational contexts and their role within society. It shows the complex relationships between children, teachers, schools, administrators, policy makers, and parents that influence teaching and learning within educational contexts.

CONSTRUCTING AND (RE)PRESENTING THE RESEARCH TEXT

An important elements of narrative constellations is the construction and (re) presentation of the research text. This is not the interview transcript, field notes or other raw data sources. Rather it is all of the data written together into a meaningful explanation of the context. Research texts "grow out of the repeated asking of questions concerning meaning and significance" (Clandinin & Connelly, 2000, p. 132). In this way, writing, too, can be viewed as an interpretative process (Ezzy, 2002). Writing must remain close to the data (Janesick, 2000) and, importantly, allow the voices of the participants to be heard (Ezzy, 2002; Goodson, 1992; Schultz, 2006) in each of their individual narrative accounts.

Research texts are usually quite large. Many of my research texts are usually between 6000–10000 words as they need to cover the complexities within educational contexts by representing children, families, teachers, principals, communities and policy makers. This can sometimes make them problematic for publication in traditional forms of journal publications that do not allow large word counts. While it is possible to publish constellations in journals (see for example Garvis & Pendergast, 2012), it is often more likely that narrative constellations are represented in book publications.

Below is a list of important areas to consider in the research text. These need to be acknowledged throughout all research texts and provide the importance of the individual and context to become known. There are:

1. The Importance of Context
According to Ezzy, "the parts of the story become significant only as they are placed within the context of the whole narrative" (2002, p. 95). Context is therefore "ever present" in narrative thinking, and includes "temporal context, spatial context, and context of other people," and its inclusion in any research text is essential for meaning-making (Clandinin & Connelly, 2000, p. 32). It is important to try and construct educational contexts in each of the narrative accounts to provide a clear understanding of the relationship between context and experience.

2. Voice
Participants' voices carry "the tone, the language, the quality, the feelings" (Butt, Raymond, McCue & Yamagishi, 1992, p. 57), informing readers not only about participants' experiences, but also about their values and beliefs. As Richardson (1990, p. 12) states, "when we write, not only do we speak about the people we study, we also speak for them. This is an important statement for the researcher to always consider. As we inscribe their lives, we bestow meaning and promulgate values", Subsequently, as Bruner (1986, p. 121) notes, "language can never be neutral" it "necessarily imposes a perspective in which things are viewed and a stance toward what we view". For this reason, I make sure that the voices of the interviewees are heard in their individual narratives (Ezzy, 2002; Goodson, 1992; Schultz, 2006). My writing has remained as close to the data as possible (Janesick, 2000). This is not an easy task and will often require a large amount of time. However the essence of

CHAPTER 2

acknowledging the importance of voice is a key characteristic of the narrative genre.

3. Cleaning the Text from Speech to Written

The spoken text of some of the participants appears inherently messy in transcripts, field notes and observations. For this reason, Elliott believes that it is preferable to "clean" or "sanitise" written texts, because it renders them easier to read, in that the focus can be on content meaning rather than on the confusion of directly transcribed verbal utterances (2005, p. 52). I personally edit some of my participants' spoken language by "adding appropriate punctuation, removing [some] pauses and false starts, and editing out [some of] the messy features of everyday speech" (Richardson, 1985, p. 137 as cited in Elliott, 2005, p. 52). I then return the original transcript to the participant for checking, to ensure that what has been changed is in agreement with the participant.

4. Changes of Fonts

In a narrative constellation, the spoken text from the interviews is interwoven with the researcher's thoughts of the story. This is an important characteristic of the narrative constellation approach. It is however important to distinguish the two sets of perspectives. In the story constellations that I have created, my thoughts are represented in Garamond font to represent my voice. I will then use *Garamond italics* to represent the direct voices of the participants. When the two are written side by side it becomes easier to see the two perspectives. Examples of the changing of the fonts is shown in chapter 5, 6 and 7 that are examples of narrative constellations.

5. Creating Belief Statements

In her story constellation methodology, Craig (2003) uses metaphors to describe the relationship between teacher knowledge, the school context and reform initiatives. The influence of the metaphor "cumulatively makes bubbles to the surface" (Craig, 2003, p. 191). Metaphors reveal educators' knowledge lived in and over the continuum on the professional knowledge landscape of each schooling context. Moreover, they provide greater understandings of the underlying tensions within the complex contexts and the influences of these on teachers. Not only are the "educators' metaphors explicitly connected to known plot lines, each carried strong moral messages as narrative phenomena are included to do" (Gudmundsdottir, 1991, cited in Craig,

18

WHAT ARE CONSTELLATION NARRATIVES?

2003, p. 198). While some researchers use metaphors, I use belief statements to conceptualise the different educational contexts. The creation of belief statements are created after a search to identify the over arching statements that capture the beliefs, perspectives and values presented. Belief statements are created after the research text has been written. They are used as headings or titles to introduce the research text and provide important perspectives to the reader. Belief statements carry critical points to the reader, helping make the excavation and establishment of meaning possible.

6. Negotiating the Research Texts

The constellation approach is always respectful of the participant. The final step in the research text is to return to the field to share the narrative accounts (story constellations) that have been written with all participants. Uncertain of how they will be interpreted, I always have some "doubt and uncertainty" on my part (Clandinin & Connelly, 2000, p. 173). I want to see how my participants would respond to the texts I have constructed (Mishler, 2004, p. 118) and if they consider a true representation of who they are. More importantly, I also want to show my respect for the participants. Many qualitative studies do not show this detail of respect to participants, with many researchers never contacting participants again once data has been collected. While this is common in some research approaches, it is also important for researchers to consider the 'coldness' of their conduct and how they may also further shape the participants understanding about researchers and research documents. I always want to create an honest and open relationship with the participants. I ask participants to respond to the questions: "Is this you? Do you see yourself here?" and, "Is this the character you want to be when this is read by others?" (Clandinin & Connelly, 2000, p. 148). It is important that participants are able to see themselves within the narratives. When all participants are happy, the research process can then proceed.

7. Leaving the Field

Part of the research approach within narrative constellations is also to acknowledge the concept of leaving the field. I believe that many researchers do not provide enough consideration to the ending of the research process and relationship. Hatch suggests (2002, p. 66) that leaving the field "is an especially sensitive issue when participants and researchers have formed close bonds" and he acknowledges that

19

CHAPTER 2

an abrupt departure from the field as "ethically unacceptable when participants have made themselves vulnerable through close personal contact with researchers". Having a close bond with the research participants can make it difficult to leave the field. I still receive occasional emails from research participants.

TRUSTWORTHINESS

According to Denzin and Lincoln (2000), for each quantitative methodological procedure for establishing reliability and validity, qualitative inquiries have aligning and parallel procedures. Trustworthiness refers to the ways in which the research may be judged to be credible, transferable, dependable and confirmable (Denzin & Lincoln, 1994; Lincoln & Guba, 1985). In a narrative constellation, these criteria to increase the trustworthiness of the research are considered throughout the research process (Harrison et al., 2001, p. 324).

Credibility

The act of attending to a study's credibility "refers to the conscious effort to establish confidence in an accurate interpretation of the meaning of the data" (Carboni, 1995, as cited in Whittemore, Chase, & Mandle, 2001, p. 530). The techniques employed in narrative constellation study to ensure this credibility are prolonged engagement, member checks, peer debriefing and triangulation of data. Spending time to build strong relationships with the participants allows proper trust to be developed, leading to more honesty, frankness, and completeness in the participants' responses (Glesne, 1999). Repeat interviews throughout the study help in developing rapport and increased the believability of the interviews (Glesne, 1999). The on-going interviews also allow the participants time to think more deeply about their own feelings, reactions, and perceptions.

After the transcription of the interviews, I check the transcription against the recordings as a step in ensuring the accuracy of the transcription. Transcripts are then returned to participants for member checking for accuracy and palatability of the data (Stake, 1995). It also gives the participants "a chance to comment and add materials, change their minds, and offer their interpretations" (Fontana & Frey, 2000, p. 751). Member checks attempt to bring the voice of the researched into the research process (Lincoln & Guba, 1985), but the researcher has the complete responsibility for the analyses and interpretation of the data.

20

WHAT ARE CONSTELLATION NARRATIVES?

I debriefed with colleagues about my narrative constellations. This increases the likelihood of producing credible findings. Unlike member checks, peer debriefing provides the perspectives of a peer who is not involved in the research project (Lincoln & Guba, 1985). Through various meetings, peer debriefing enabled me to question methods, assumptions and representations throughout the study. Credibility id also improved by using structural corroboration, a qualitative parallel to triangulation, called structural collaboration.

Transferability

The design of most qualitative studies has a focus on particularity, and does not usually attempt to be generalisable (Maxwell, 2002; Seale, 1999). Therefore, the point has been made that, rather than being an issue for researchers, transferability is an issue for readers, who assume the responsibility of deciding whether any study can contribute meaningfully to the contexts of their own study (Burns, 2000; Lincoln & Guba, 1985). While I try to demonstrate greater insight and understanding about the phenomenon, readers must make their own judgment regarding the applicability of this study in their own context (Seale, 1999).

Dependability

To improve dependability, I create an audit trail. It consists of well maintained careful documentation of field notes, audio files, transcriptions and data analyses. This lay open for inspection of "the researchers' documentation of data, methods and decisions made during a project, as well as its end product" (Seale, 1999; Lincoln & Guba, 1985). The aim of an audit trail is to leave behind "footprints to allow others to judge the utility of the work, and to profit from it" (Huberman & Miles, 2002, p. x). Every month I would review the audit trail.

Confirmability

The confirmability of qualitative research parallels the objectivity of quantitative research (Denzin & Lincoln, 2000). Any research based on the recollection of a participant within a study is ultimately a study of perceptions, therefore "in valuing the first-person account, one must equally assume certain unknowns" (Huberman, 1993, p. 22). Data comfirmability is ensured through structural corroboration of multiple sources (interviews,

21

CHAPTER 2

field notes and observations) and using member check, peer debriefing and the co-construction of narratives.

Structural Corroboration

Historically, researchers have used *triangulation* as a means to improve the validity of studies. Triangulation is the process of using multiple reference points to establish a singular "truth" (Denscombe, 1998; Richardson, 2000). It is used by positivist case study researchers to verify and confirm their findings before offering them for widespread dissemination, review and reaction (Hancock & Algozzine, 2006).

I choose to use a qualitative alternative to triangulation, known as 'structural corroboration' (Eisner, 1991). According to Eisner (1991) *structural corroboration* is a criterion for assessing coherence. 'Structural corroboration occurs when multiple types of data are related to each other to support or contradict the interpretation and evaluation of a state of affairs' (Eisner, 1991, p. 110).

In my narrative constellations I use 'multiple forms of data' to 'structurally corroborate' interpretations. Often meaningful connections are made between my field notes of participants in and their accounts during interviews. These corroborations assist a broader interpretation of the beliefs, values and experiences of each participant.

REFLEXIVITY AND SUBJECTIVITY

In narrative constellations, I examine and discolse my own reflexivity on my research. I believe that "subjective researchers cannot separate themselves from the phenomena and people they study" (Toma, 2000, p. 178). Unravelling what we bring to the research in terms of our own biographies, "our emotions, intuitions, experiences, meanings, values, commitments, presuppositions, prejudices and personal agendas" (Finlay & Gough, 2003, p. 40), biases and baggage, the limitations of understanding and their influence on our data interpretation, is crucial to producing trustworthy qualitative writing (Ely, Vinz, Downing, & Anzul, 1997; Finlay, 2003; Josselson, 2007).

Like Kvale's (1996, p. 4) "traveller metaphor", I explore different contexts entering into conversations with the many particiapnts encountered. Conversing with these participants in the "original Latin meaning of *conversation* as *wandering together with*" (Kvale, 1996, p. 4), the journey leads not only to new knowledge, but instigates a process of reflection creating new ways of understanding the phenomenon. As Russell and Kelly

22

(2002, p. 11) suggest, "when we are reflexive, other human participants join us in being reflective as well".

My approach became that of a "virtuous researcher" as being "synonymous with thinking critically about one's research practices …wherein one identifies possible sources for the anxiety of influence" (Maton, 2003, p. 55). I decided to write myself into the text, becoming a visible partner in the co-constructed narratives. I subsequently find myself to be inextricably part of the research process (Mantzoukas, 2004). I become "the research instrument" (Gilbert, 2001, p. 4; see also Josselson, 2007). I realise that I am grounded in all parts of the research, including choices about methodology, data generation methods, subject selection, data selection, analysis and interpretation (Finlay, 2003; Gough, 2003).

My voice becomes present everywhere – "overarching and undergirding the text, framing the piece, naming the metaphors and echoing through the central themes" (Lawrence-Lightfoot & Davis, 1997, p. 85). My voice reflects my interest in authorship, interpretation, relationship, aesthetics and the narratives. I always attempt to demonstrate the extent of my reflexivity by incorporating useful contextual information, and allowing readers access to my relevant cognitive and affective responses throughout this research text (Gough, 2003). Consequently, readers will be able to evaluate for themselves "the adequacy of the methods employed" in this study (Stevenson & Cooper, 1997, p. 160).

LIMITATIONS

While the narrative constellations illuminate participants' unfolding contextualized experiences over time, they do not produce "a script to be followed nor plans to be implemented" (Davis, Jr., 2003, p. ii). The constellations only provide snapshots of the teller of that story. They operate in a Bakhtinian spirit of *novelness*, where they may "inspire readers to enter into dialogue with them" (Barone & Eisner, 1997, p. 75). The narratives avoid the *epic* texts approach where the purpose is "to impart the final word, to shut out other voices, to close down interpretive options" (Barone & Eisner, 1997, p. 75).

CONCLUSION

This chapter has shown the importance of narrative constellations in research and provided detailes about the research process. This has included a focus on data collection, research text, and the validity of the data. In any narrative

CHAPTER 2

constellation it is important to also engage in a reflexive approach to continuously question all stages and analysis. It is important for continual critical reflection in a narrative constellation. The next chapter provides an examples of a narrative constellation.

REFERENCES

Barone, T. (2001). *Touching eternity: The enduring outcomes of teaching*. New York, NY: Teachers College Press.

Barone, T., & Eisner, E. W. (1997). Arts-based educational research. In R. M. Jaeger (Ed.), *Complementary methods for research in education* (2nd ed.). Washington, DC: AERA.

Barrett, M. S., & Smigiel, H. (2003). Awakening the 'Sleeping giant: The arts in the lives of Australian families.' *International Journal of Education & the Arts, 4* [Online]. Retrieved July 4, 2008, from http://www.ijea.org/v4n4/index.html (Accessed November 10, 2008)

Bennett, K. P., & LeCompte, M. D. (1990). *The way schools work: A sociological analysis of education*. New York, NY: Longman.

Bogdan, R. C., & Biklen, S. K. (1998). *Qualitative research for education: An introduction to theory and methods*. Needham Heights, MA: Ally & Bacon.

Bruner, J. S. (1986). *Actual minds, possible worlds*. Cambridge, MA: Harvard University Press.

Burns, R. B. (2000). *Introduction to research methods* (4th ed.). London, UK: Sage.

Butt, D., Raymond, D., McCue, G., & Yamagishi, L. (1992). Collaborative autobiography and the teacher's voice. In I. F. Goodson (Ed.), *Studying teachers' lives* (pp. 51–98). London, UK: Routledge.

Carter, K. (1993). The place of story in the study of teaching and teacher education. *Educational Researcher, 22*(1), 5–12.

Chambliss, D. F., & Schutt, R. K. (2003). *Making sense of the social world: Methods of investigation*. Thousand Oaks, CA: Sage.

Clandinin, D. J., & Connelly, F. M. (1994). Personal experience methods. In N. K. Denzin & Y. S. Lincoln (Eds.), *Handbook of qualitative research* (pp. 413–427). Thousand Oaks, CA: Sage.

Clandinin, D. J., & Connelly, F. M. (2000). *Narrative inquiry*. San Francisco, CA: Jossey-Bass.

Craig, C. J. (2001). Relationships between and among teacher knowledge, communities of knowing, and top-down school reform: A case of "the Monkey's Paw". *Curriculum Inquiry, 31*(3), 303–331.

Craig, C. J. (2003) School portfolio development: A teacher knowledge approach. *Journal of Teacher Education, 54*(2), 122–135.

Craig, C. (2007). Story constellations: A narrative approach to situating teachers' knowledge of school reform in context. *Teaching and Teacher Education, 23*(2), 173–188. '

Crites, S. (1975). Angels we have heard. In J. B. Wiggins (Ed.), *Religion as story* (pp. 23–63). Lanham, MD: University Press of America.

Davis, O. L. Jr. (2003). Foreword. In C. J. Craig (Ed.), *Narrative inquiries of school reform. Storied lives, storied landscapes, storied metaphors*. Greenwich, CT: Information Age Publishing.

Denscombe, M. (1998). *The good research guide for small-scale social research projects.* Buckingham, UK: Open University Press.

Denzin, N. K., & Lincoln, Y. S. (Eds.). (2000). *Handbook of qualitative research* (2nd ed.). Thousand Oaks, CA: Sage.

Easton, K. L., McComish, J. F., & Greenberg, R. (2000). Avoiding common pitfalls in qualitative data collection and transcription. *Qualitative Health Research, 10*(5), 703–707.

Eisner, E. W. (1991). *The enlightened eye: Qualitative inquiry and the enhancement of educational practice.* New York, NY: Macmillan.

Elliott, J. (2005). *Using narrative in social research: Qualitative and quantitative approaches.* London, UK: Sage.

Ely, M., Vinz, R., Downing, M., & Anzul, M. (1997). *On writing qualitative research: Living by words.* London, UK: Falmer Press.

Ezzy, D. (2002). *Qualitative analysis: Practice and innovation.* Crows Nest, NSW, Australia: Allen & Unwin.

Finlay, L. (2003). The reflexive journey: Mapping multiple routes. In L. Finlay & B. Gough (Eds.), *Reflexivity: A practical guide for researchers in health and social sciences* (pp. 3–20). Oxford, UK: Blackwell Science.

Finlay, L., & Gough, B. (Eds.). (2003). *Reflexivity: A practical guide for researchers in health and social sciences.* Oxford, UK: Blackwell Science.

Fontana, A., & Frey, J. H. (1998). Interviewing: The art of science. In N. Denzin & Y. Lincoln (Eds.), *Collecting and interpreting qualitative materials* (pp. 47–78). Thousand Oaks, CA: Sage.

Fontana, A., & Frey, J. H. (2000). The interview: From structured questions to negotiated text. In N. K. Denzin & Y. S. Lincoln (Eds.), *Handbook of qualitative research.* Thousand Oaks, CA: Sage.

Garvis, S. (2010). *An investigation of beginning teacher self-efficacy for the arts in the middle years of schooling (years 4–9)* [PhD Thesis]. Queensland, Australia: School of Music, University of Queensland.

Garvis, S., & Pendergast, D. (2012). Storying music and the arts education: The generalist teacher voice. *British Journal of Music Education, 29*(1), 57–75.

Gilbert, K. R. (2001). *The emotional nature of qualitative research.* Boca Raton, FL: CRC Press.

Glesne, C. (1999). *Becoming qualitative researchers.* New York, NY: Longman.

Goodson, I. F. (1992). Sponsoring the teacher's voice: Teachers' lives and teacher development. In A. Hargreaves & M. G. Fullan (Eds.), *Understanding teacher development* (pp. 110–121). London, UK: Cassell.

Gough, B. (2003). Deconstructing reflexivity. In L. Finlay & B. Gough (Eds.), *Reflexivity: A practical guide for researchers in health and social sciences* (pp. 21–38). Oxford, UK: Blackwell Science.

Gubrium, J. F., & Holstein, J. A. (Eds.). (2002). *Handbook of interview research: Context and method.* Thousand Oaks, CA: Sage.

Hatch, J. A. (2002). *Doing qualitative research in educational settings.* Albany, NY: State University of New York.

Hancock, D. R., & Algozzine, B. (2006). *Doing case study research: A practical guide for beginning researchers.* New York, NY: Teachers College Press.

CHAPTER 2

Harrison, J., MacGibbon, L., & Morton, M. (2001). Regimes of trustworthiness in qualitative research: The rigors of reciprocity. *Qualitative Inquiry, 7*(3), 323–345.

Huber, J., & Whelan, K. (2001). Beyond the still pond: Community as growing edges. *Reflective practice, 2*, 221–236.

Huberman, M. (1993). Linking the practitioner and researcher communities for school improvement. *School Effectiveness and School Improvement, 4*, 1–16.

Huberman, A. M., & Miles, M. B. (Eds.). (2002). *The qualitative researcher's companion.* Thousand Oaks, CA: Sage.

Husserl, E. (1965) *Philosophy as a rigorous science in phenomenology and the crisis of philosophy* (Q. Lauer, Trans., pp. 71–147). New York, NY: Harper & Row.

Kirkevold, M., & Bergland, A. (2007). The quality of qualitative data: Issues to consider when interviewing participants who have difficulties providing detailed accounts of their experiences. *International Journal of Qualitative Studies on Health and Well-Being, 2*(2), 68–75.

Kvale, S. (1996). *Interviews: An introduction to qualitative research interviewing.* London, UK: Sage.

Janesick, V. (1994). The dance of qualitative research design: Metaphor, methodolatry, and meaning. In N. K. Denzin & Y. S. Lincoln (Eds.), *Handbook of qualitative research* (pp. 209–235). Thousand Oaks, CA: Sage.

Janesick, V. (2000). The choreography of qualitative research design: Minuets, improvisations, and crystallization. In N. K. Denzin & Y. S. Lincoln (Eds.), *Handbook of qualitative research* (2nd ed., pp. 379–400). Thousand Oaks, CA: Sage.

Josselson, R. (2007). The ethical attitude in narrative research: Principles and practicalities. In D. J. Clandinin (Ed.), *Handbook of narrative inquiry: Mapping a methodology* (pp. 537–566). Thousand Oaks, CA: Sage.

Lawrence-Lightfoot, S., & Davis, H. J. (1997). *The art and science of portraiture.* San Francisco, CA: Jossey-Bass.

Lincoln, Y. S., & Guba, E. G. (1985). *Naturalistic inquiry.* Beverly Hills, CA: Sage.

Mantzoukas, S. (2004). Issues of representation within qualitative inquiry. *Qualitative Health Research, 14*(7), 994–1007.

Mason, B. L. (1998). E-Texts: The orality and literacy issue revisited. *Oral Tradition, 13*(2), 306–329.

Maton, K. (2003). Reflexivity, relationism and research. *Space and Culture, 6*(1), 52–65.

Maxwell, J. A. (2002). Understanding and validity in qualitative research. In A. M. Huberman & M. B. Miles (Eds.), *The qualitative researcher's companion* (pp. 37–64). Thousand Oaks, CA: Sage.

Mishler, E. G. (2004). Historians of the self: Restorying lives, revising identities. *Research in Human Development, 1*(1 & 2), 101–121.

Polkinghorne, D. E. (1988). *Narrative knowing and the human sciences.* Albany, NY: State of New York University Press.

Richardson, L. (2000). Writing: A method of inquiry. In N. K. Denzin & Y. S. Lincoln (Eds.), *Handbook of qualitative research* (2nd ed., pp. 923–943). Thousand Oaks, CA: Sage.

Richardson, L. (1990). *Writing strategies: Reaching diverse audiences.* Thousand Oaks, CA: Sage.

Rosenthal, G. (1993). Reconstruction of life stories: Principles of selection in generating stories for narrative biographical interviews. In R. Josselson & A. Lieblich (Eds.), *The narrative study of lives* (Vol. 1, pp. 59–91). Newbury Park, CA: Sage.

Russell, G. M., & Kelly, N. H. (2002). Research as interacting dialogic processes: Implications for reflexivity. *Forum for Qualitative Social Research, 3(3), Art. 18* [Online]. Retrieved June 3, 2008, from http://nbn-resolving.de/urn:nbn:de:0114-fqs0203181

Schultz, B. D. (2006). Not satisfied with stupid band-aids: A portrait of a justice-oriented, democratic curriculum serving a disadvantaged neighbourhood. *Equity & Excellence in Education, 40*(2), 166–176.

Schwandt, T. A. (1994). Constructivist, interpretivist approaches to human inquiry. In N. K. Denzin & Y. S. Lincoln (Eds.), *Handbook of qualitative research* (pp. 118–137). Thousand Oaks, CA: Sage.

Seale, C. (1999). *The quality of qualitative research*. London, UK: Sage.

Seidman, I. E. (1991). *Interviewing as qualitative research*. New York, NY: Teachers College Press.

Stake, R. E. (1995). *The art of case research*. Thousand Oaks, CA: Sage Publications.

Stevenson, C., & Cooper, N. (1997). Qualitative and quantitative research. *The Psychologist: Bulletin of the British Psychological Society, 10*, 159–160.

Teeravarunyou, S., & Sato, K. (2001). *Object-mediated user knowledge elicitation method.* Proceedings of the 5th Asian Design Research Conference, Seoul, Korea.

Toma, J. D. (2000). How getting close to your subjects makes qualitative data better. *Theory into Practice, 39*(3), 177–184 [Online]. Retrieved October 30, 2009, from http://links.jstor.org/sici?sici=0040-5841%28200022%2939%3A3%3C177%3AHGCTYS%3E2.0.CO%3B2-H

Whittemore, R., Chase, S. K., & Mandle, C. L., (2001). Validity in qualitative research. *Qualitative Health Research, 11*, 522–537.

CHAPTER 3

AT THIS SCHOOL ARTS EDUCATION IS TRAVELLING ON A ROCKY ROAD

INTRODUCTION

Chapter three shares the story constellation from a one-teacher school in Australia, highlighting the differences in educational contexts. The intention is to show the reader what a story constellation looks like, as well as to understand how story constellations can show the complexities between values, beliefs and perspectives.

This story constellation examines the lived experiences of Tabitha Jones, a third year teacher who is also the principal of a rural one teacher school. It explores her daily struggles with teaching arts education against the backdrop of state and national reform in curriculum. It also probes those beliefs and values associated with rural stereotypes, teaching the arts and current support structures. From this context emerges the value statement "at this school arts education is travelling on a rocky road".

INTRODUCING TABITHA'S ONE TEACHER RURAL SCHOOL

Tabitha Jones lives in a small rural town in outback Queensland. The rural community is a fifteen hour bus trip west of Brisbane. It is not easily accessible. The bus service operates only on Monday, Thursday and Saturday. By road, you generally need a 4WD[1] for some of the dirt roads. Without a regular air service, flying in and out is also not a possibility. Consequently I talk with Tabitha regularly over the phone and email.

Since I am unable to physically visit this small rural community, I decide to gain a virtual understanding of the rural context from the internet. I type in the town's name and wait for Google[2] to respond. Up pop 15,000 results. I click on the first few websites with my trusty mouse.

The town itself has a population of around 40 people, servicing local sheep and cattle properties. It was founded around 1862 and became a Cobb and Co depot, where horses were changed and rested. I look at an old black

CHAPTER 3

and white photo on one website, admiring the pioneers who travelled rural Queensland in horse and wagon. In those days, this town was the hub of life for the many sheep and cattle properties.

I look at current photos of the town. It appears a mere skeleton of its former self. It consists of a cafe (that doubles as a post office), hotel and houses. The closest bank is a 45 minute drive to a larger town. According to one website, occasional film crews see the place as ideal for shooting movies based in isolated Australia. Another website suggests it can cater for any film crew with food and accommodation. I wonder where and how?

I find an online photo of the small main street. The landscape is desolate and barren. There is no guttering on the street curb and the old road is flat. Parts of the bitumen are falling away into the ground. I start to think there is something missing … what is it … I look harder … oh yes … grass and greenery. It is absent in the swell of red dirt and dust.

In the middle of the photo stands the old pub (hotel). It consists of four wood walls, with a wrap around balcony to keep out the summer's heat. On the tin roof appears a XXXX sign[3], showing loyalty to the Australian beer company.

After a search through my Google results on the laptop, I come across this hotel's website. Opening hours are advertised as "open all day, every day of the year" (www.de-identified.com.au, accessed 12 March 2009). The hotel also advertises fine Australian cuisine. It offers food such as emu, kangaroo, or wallaby combined with native herbs, fruits and vegetables sourced locally whenever possible. One of the most popular bar menu items is listed as the 'feral mixed grill[4] '(www.de-identified.com.au, 12 March 2009). I make a mental note that if I ever visited this place, I would have to try the local cuisine.

I continue with my online tour. The town has had a school for 150 years. The building however is only 100 years old. It consists of a one-classroom building that was built in the typical architecture of Queensland schools from that period of early twentieth century colonisation. The building sits firmly on cement stilts, allowing airflow on the hot summer afternoons. The area underneath the building is used for student morning teas and lunches. A small playing field for students sits behind the building. The grass (I finally find something green!) struggles to survive amongst the red dirt. Recently, the Parents and Citizens Association improved the outdoor area by fundraising and building a combined tennis and basketball court (www.de-identified. com.au, accessed 12 March 2009).

(The one school building, 2009)

Nine students attend the small rural school (seven boys and two girls) in a variety of year levels from prep to year seven. The majority of students are from farming properties. Without a bus service, parents drive their children long distances to attend school. For one student, the daily commute from the farm is too far. He boards with a local family through the week and returns home on the weekend.

The school prides itself on having access to 'state of the art' technology for students. In its annual school report (2008[5]), it claims that 'there was one computer for every two students'. This is further complemented by a range of peripheral information technology equipment such as a digital camera, digital video camera, teleconferencing facility, colour printer, scanner and data projector. To the school, technology is evidently an important link to the outside world. For the students, it also provides access to specialist lessons. Every week, students have a thirty minute LOTE (Language Other Than English) lesson via a teleconference. Students talk directly with a language specialist from the School of Distance Education[6].

I ask Tabitha Jones to email photos from her classroom to gain a better understanding of her multi-age classroom. It currently consists of ten desks with blue chairs. At the back of the room is a pin board with a display about the current unit 'Our World'. This unit is designed to teach students about different countries and cultures. In the middle of the display hangs a blow-up globe where students can locate each of the continents.

(Current display in the classroom, 2009)

CHAPTER 3

TEACHER STORY

Tabitha Jones is in her mid 30s. She has always taught in rural schools. In her first year of teaching, she taught at a two-teacher school in far west Queensland. In her second year, she was a beginning teacher principal at a school for three students. The school closed at the end of the schooling year, forcing Tabitha to relocate to her current position. Tabitha now resides in town near the school, and is hoping to stay in the community for more than a year. She speaks familiarly about the people, places and events as though they are her own community. Upon further questioning, I discover that even though she grew up eight hours from where she is now teaching, she is friends with members of the local community. I am reminded of the vast distances people in remote Queensland travel to interact.

In my first interview with Tabitha, I sit waiting for the clock to tick over before I dial the number on the cordless conference phone. Tick, tick tick ... 8.30am had just ticked over. I press the numbers on the phone keypad. Beep, beep, beep ...

(My phone communication, 2009)

A friendly voice answers the phone. *"Oh hi Susie. Can you ring back in 5 minutes. I just need to talk to the supply teacher quickly"*. I recall it is Thursday, the day when Tabitha has a supply teacher to relieve her in some of her teaching duties. I hang up.

Ten minutes later I ring back to be greeted by her friendly voice. *"OK great! I am a little excited about being interviewed"*. I turn on the recorder ready to begin my questions. Initially, I want to find out about Tabitha's previous experiences with the arts.

I take a deep breath and begin. "Could you tell me about your experiences with the arts, starting from childhood". Tabitha begins immediately, eager to share her experience.

I Was Home Schooled for Most of Primary School

Well as a child, formal arts education we really didn't have. I was home schooled. We lived out on a property so I was home schooled for virtually all of my primary schooling. Arts wasn't really my Mum's strong point, so we simply didn't do art lessons. She pauses before continuing. But I was lucky that I came from a very crafty family. My Mum loved sewing and my grandmothers loved sewing so I got taught too. Well they tried to teach me to knit but that didn't really work but I got taught to spin and sew at a very young age. My grandmothers would get into various art fads so I got taught to make pictures out of wool – all those sorts of things. We really didn't have a formal arts education in primary school though.

When I went to boarding school for my high school years, it was compulsory to do visual arts in grade eight and I think because I didn't have the skills from primary school my art was so terrible. I only did it in year 8.

I anticipate that Tabitha's experience with the arts would end there. She draws in a breath before continuing to explain her involvement in extra-curricula experiences.

When I was at boarding school though, I did a lot of stage management, lighting, props, as well as acting ... And I hit uni[versity] and that was it. No more. I mean I still kept up the sewing and various sorts of art like jewellery ... but I don't make jewellery anymore, mostly because the craft shop has closed down.

Tabitha becomes silent on the phone. What is happening? Twenty seconds slips by. Tabitha begins again and in my head, I sigh with relief.

This time her voice is softer and slower. I move the recorder closer to the phone to make sure it records. Tabitha begins telling me her secret pain of broken dreams for the theatre.

Broken Dreams for the Theatre

I just wasn't allowed. It broke my heart.

Tabitha was not able to pursue her dream of working in the theatre after she had left boarding school. To her farming parents, the theatre *was an extracurricular activity that could be pursued anytime outside of a career.* They would not support her financially in a theatre course. Defeated, Tabitha turned to primary school teaching as a backup plan. She could *easily get a job* and she had *the right entry level score to get in.*

CHAPTER 3

Tabitha describes her first year of university as *chaotic*. She did not like university or studying education. Rather she *mucked around, pulled out* and *ended up working overseas in hospitality.* Tabitha again hesitates on the phone line before continuing.

I mean it is alright in a short burst, but I just don't like hospitality. I returned to Australia and went to the bush[7] for work. I worked with a rural church organisation that provided parent support groups and children's playgroups in the Cape York[8]. From these experiences working with rural communities, Tabitha felt a reconnection with teaching children and a passion for rural education. This prompted her to enrol in university externally to finish her teaching degree.

During this period she discusses learning the basics about arts education at university. However she admits, *six years down the track you can't really remember too much so it didn't really help much. What I teach kids now are things I learnt from running the children's playgroups.* Tabitha feels she does not have adequate content knowledge from university to teach arts education at school.

I ask Tabitha if she misses the theatre. She takes a deep, slow breath. It echoes down the phone.

I used to ...

I mean I used to miss it. I think it's gotten to the point where I'm pretty much out of practice ... I also find it difficult doing theatre activities with young kids at school ... I struggle with teaching it. It wasn't touched on in uni[versity] either. I struggle trying to figure out how to teach the basics of theatre. And I get a bit frustrated trying to teach it. For me, theatre and acting are things that are fairly easy to do. But teaching it is one thing I have troubles with. Acting yes, teaching [acting] no.

Quick Rise to Becoming a Principal

Tabitha is highly ambitious. She had applied to become a principal within the first two years of her teaching career, even though it was not policy. She became a teacher two years after graduating from teacher education. Since she was an older beginning teacher (in her thirties) she wanted to *catch up* on the career ladder.

Well technically you're not supposed to apply to be a principal until you've done two years of teaching at a regular school. And even then, most teachers don't tend to apply until they've done three or four years of teaching. I did one year of teaching.

34

According to Tabitha, it was a time of enormous change as she had to balance teaching responsibilities with principal responsibilities within her one teacher school. Tabitha begins to realise that her ambitions may also have outstripped her capacity for teaching. In hindsight, Tabitha suggests it *was probably not a good idea to go into a principal position* as she still struggles *with the teaching side. It was stressful.* She pauses. I wait quietly, staring at the cordless conference phone. Thoughts run through my head. Does she really feel like she is struggling with teaching? I wait.

You know I still struggle with trying to cater for the learning needs of the students with all different ages and abilities. The school I'm at, independent learning doesn't quite work. The students have, for lack of a better way of putting it, been babied over the years. I have about four students who won't pick up a pencil unless you sit beside them. If you move away from their side, down goes the pencil and they stop work until you come back and sit beside them. They don't need help, they're just not used to working independently.

I seem to have spent most of this term without too much success trying to train the kids into working on their own so that I can spend quality time with each of the group. Once they're got that, it'll be a lot easier. But right at the moment I'm pulling my hair out and they're not happy either.

My Ideal Day

Over the course of our interviews, I notice that Tabitha is unhappy with her current school context. She sees various school problems as contributors to her lack of engaging with arts activities in the classroom.

The first is the school's layout. Tabitha describes the one-room classroom *as small and without having suitable lino space.* To Tabitha, it is highly inappropriate for arts activities. Next, Tabitha expresses further reluctance to engage with visual arts activities *since the school is without a permanent cleaner.* Cleaning is currently done by volunteers from the local community. Tabitha does *not want to scare them off by massive, regular messes when the floor is only cleaned once a week.*

Tabitha voices her concerns about suitable administrative staff. She finds administrative support vital to the overall *day to day running of the school.*

Some schools have really good administration officers, I had a really good one at my last school who covered a lot of things. You know I'd just have to say 'that bloody computer's dying' and she'd be on the computer and she would have found you 'this is a good one to replace it' and 'yes we've got money in the budget' or 'no we can't but, if we take money out of this section

CHAPTER 3

then yes we can replace this computer'. She was really good, but she went above and beyond what was required of her for that job.

The administration officer I've got now doesn't do that, she comes in part time. She's here two days, well two half days a week, but it's just simple things. It's staffing problems that we've had with her in previous years – she's not at work today and I got an email about half an hour ago saying she wasn't coming to work. She should have been here at eight o'clock.

She's been away for a year so we're struggling to get her back into following her role and doing what it is that she's supposed to be doing. There are things that because she had so much time off last year she's struggling to work the various computer programs and systems that we need to run the school. She's having difficulty with them. She's not up-to-date on the appropriate forms and things like that. So a lot of the stuff that she does I then have to re-do the following day when we get the email or the faxes through saying that you did it wrong. So that for me is fairly frustrating but I'm hoping that with time you know she'll catch herself up and things will get a bit better.

Establishing regular routines for students is also difficult. At the drop of a hat, the school day can change if Tabitha is interrupted by principal business. For example, if the phone rings and an activity is outside, the students may need to go back inside with Tabitha as there is no extra supervision after the teacher aide leaves.

The phone interruptions are constant so well, quite often the phone gets locked in a room where I can't hear it, and then we sort of kind of got to try and listen out for it because the parents have realized that I won't answer the phone during school lessons if I can help it. So they've got to the point where they'll ring and hang up and then ring and hang up and then ring and hang up and then ring again, and by that time I would have got the hint there's someone that desperately needs to get in touch with me. I'll answer it [the phone] and it will be 'ohh yeah I'm not picking so-and-so up until such-and-such a time' or 'this one needs to go to a doctor's appointment in half an hour I'm coming over'. Really disruptive.

Tabitha also speaks about the problem with student attendance. *Students are required to help with farm work during school time. Students can be gone for days at a time, especially if the family is mustering. I mean sometimes I've only got half a class. It's a bit hard because I can't really go and teach new concepts because they'll need to be re-taught again. Unfortunately, it's usually the struggling half of the class that heads off mustering.*

"So what would your ideal school day be?" I ask, hoping to find a solution to her problem.

36

Well for starters, my ideal school day would be everybody showing up for school and everybody showing up for work (cleaner, teacher aide and administrative assistant) and no interruptions at all! Then maybe I could teach the arts.

SCHOOL STORY

When Tabitha started at her current school, she became aware of current action plans for rural education. The *Rural and Remote Education Framework for Action 2006-2008* provided guidelines for adequate standards for rural education. It began with the statement:

Our Government wants to ensure that all students – no matter where they live – can pursue the educational pathways necessary to foster lifelong learning and realise their aspirations. A high-quality education and training system that meets the needs of rural and remote Queenslanders is vital for the State's future prosperity and community wellbeing. (Queensland Government, p. ii)

This framework has been adapted in different ways by various rural districts. In Tabitha's district, schools share lesson plans and resources to reduce isolation between teaching staff. It was hoped that such an approach would allow quality learning opportunities for students.

Two initiatives were encouraged to promote rural education in the district. The first initiative was allowing teachers at rural primary schools greater access to relief time. As Tabitha explains:

The district was great in changing staffing. The high schools had relinquished some of their teachers. The money that would normally go to paying those teachers is now used to pay relief staff and extra staff for the primary school. Rather than having our own little pool of supply teachers, we actually have a permanent staff of supply teachers that go around to the schools. District office actually volunteered these relief teachers to help us so we could have planning time.

Tabitha values this support and planning initiative. A relief teacher visits Tabitha one day a week and takes music, sport and technology lessons. With *constant interruptions with the phone ringing* (there was also an answering machine) *and principal duties requiring immediate attention,* Tabitha suggests it would be difficult without the support of a relief teacher one day a week. While there is a teacher aide, she is only there for the morning. *Relief time was vital.*

CHAPTER 3

The second initiative within the district consisted of the creation of a learning community. The premise of the initiative was for schools to "work together with its local communities to create and maintain sustainable structures which foster lifelong learners who have developed appropriate academic and social skills" (de-identified School Report, 2008). The learning community lists the following goals as part of its initiative (www. de-identified.com.au, accessed 14 March, 2009[9]);

(1) a shared approach to curriculum, teaching, assessment and reporting, (2) partnerships between district schools and their communities; (3) moderating students work and working in the environment of our small schools. The group believes that "through working together we free up people's time which can be better spent focusing on teaching our kids." (Website, 2009)

The group of schools (one or two teacher schools) that I'm with, there's thirteen schools now, we're actually planning units of work based around Essential Learning Statements. And to get that done and get it done efficiently, what we've done is divided it up into subject groups. I was actually in the science subject group, so I've spent the last year planning two major units of work based around science. I haven't really looked at the arts because that's another group of teachers. I'll be handed the arts lessons to teach some time before term four and I'll be able to figure it all out. Well it'll be mostly explained what I've got to teach and what activities I can use to teach this particular concept.

We're lucky I think in that we're sort of a pet project of our Executive Director. You know she's very supportive of one and two teacher schools. So we are pretty lucky in that we do have maybe more support than other schools in our situation.

The sharing of lesson plans is valued by Tabitha. If she does not understand the arts lessons, she can ring up the person who created the unit. She likes that the arts unit (like all subject units) will be taught at exactly the same time across the district. To Tabitha, this helps *reduce the isolation.*

It's Good Enough for the Country

Tabitha is keen to share her experiences with music specialists. She brings up the issue of specialist teachers having pre-conceived ideas about country folk. To Tabitha, it is important to discuss the misconception of *country folk being dumb.* She believes some music teachers think country students are not as capable as students in the city.

38

Even some specialist music teachers that we've had out here that I've seen in various schools aren't that good. I think they sort of wing it and think 'oh you know, no one else will know'.

Unfortunately it sort of backfired on one music teacher that I know. She specialised in music teaching and she decided that teaching one concept to the kids was just too hard so she wouldn't bother, she'd just tell them it meant something else. It was something to do with music notes and I think this particular note had eight or twelve beats or something and she decided that'd be too difficult for the kids to do so she told them it meant four, not taking into account she had three kids in that class who took private music lessons, who did exams and knew better. So then we had all the parents in uproar that she wasn't teaching the kids.

I don't think people really take it seriously enough and I know some music teachers who just think 'I know what I'm doing and nobody else knows what I'm doing so I can just get away with whatever out here'. You know we're not as dumb as you think. We may not have music experts or anything or visual arts experts or perceived experts, but there's a lot of talent. Be honest with what you're teaching. Don't teach crap[10] basically. If it's not true, don't teach it, be accurate in what you're teaching. These kids deserve to have a go and there's a lot of talent out there. You've just got to go to some of the local art galleries or the local craft shops to see the talent that the people in the rural areas have. So don't write us off just because there isn't a formal art gallery or formal performance theatre around.

Tabitha no longer has a music specialist to teach her students. Rather, the relief teacher is in charge of delivering the thirty minute music lesson. Tabitha is happy that she is the third school that the relief teacher visits in the week. *The relief teacher is teaching the exact lessons to three schools over the week and we are the last. The music lesson is pretty much well rehearsed by then.* According to Tabitha, she is *the luckiest out of the three schools.*

After a short pause, Tabitha comments on the problems of trying to find specialist music teachers in rural areas. *They just aren't around.* She lets out a long sigh. Since they could not find a specialist music teacher, they decided to make it a duty of the relief teacher. Tabitha discusses the problems of trying *to find a relief teacher who felt comfortable with taking music at each of the schools.*

"What about other rural principals?" I ask.

Well you know if it wasn't compulsory, some principals would throw up their hands and the kids would miss out [on music and the arts] altogether.

CHAPTER 3

CURRICULUM STORY

The district has decided to focus on literacy and numeracy initiatives, based on involvement with a project initiative in 2005. Since then, stronger pressure has also come for increased literacy and numeracy teaching from the National assessment plan for literacy and numeracy.

I ask Tabitha how she defines key learning areas within the curriculum (literacy, numeracy and the arts) to gain a better understanding of how these definitions shape her practice. Tabitha links each area with subject disciplines.

Well literacy for me is in every aspect of the classroom and of the school day. It's anything to do with reading and writing so I don't really agree with it. I have English lessons, not literacy lessons because English lessons are your grammar and writing, your reading strategies, your spelling, all those sorts of things.

Numeracy is similar. But for me, I find it difficult to get numeracy into every aspect of all the lessons so I know in my head there's a difference between numeracy and maths but transferring the numeracy learning into areas of English and the arts I find difficult. It seems to slot in a lot more easily into areas like science and maths for me.

Now the arts ...That is difficult. The arts are anything to do with performance, whether it's music, speaking, debating, giving orals, teacher production, poetry recitals. It is anything to do with visual arts so when the kids read a book, they [then] have to draw a picture or something that has happened in the book. That for me is literacy in the arts.

Tabitha's definition of the arts does not include creativity. Rather, there is a strong focus on the notion of performance. My mind races. I consider that even drawing a picture is a 'performance' of understanding what happened in the book.

I continue our interview. "So how do you use the arts in your classroom?" I ask.

Tabitha suggests that the arts are a *Friday afternoon activity, a reward for students or a lesson filler*. She justifies her teaching practice by talking about the low status of the arts in schooling. She relates it back to her lack of experience and confidence, showing snapshots of low teacher self-efficacy.

Unfortunately, I think for most people, the arts in education is just that – a fun bludge lesson you do on Friday afternoons to get the kids off your back when all you want to do is go down to the pub. I don't think it's really taken seriously. I don't think the benefits of the arts are taken advantage of enough and I think a lot of that comes down to our lack of experience and lack of confidence.

AT THIS SCHOOL ARTS EDUCATION IS TRAVELLING ON A ROCKY ROAD

I mean sometimes it's just something that you give to the kids, you know you've got to do art so let's just go and paint this picture. We won't talk to the kids about or show them any pictures that other artists have done of a similar sort, using similar mediums. We won't talk to them about colour, we won't teach them any of that. We'll just get them to paint this picture and do this activity and they'll all end up with exactly the same picture at the end of it because they've all done what they've been told. I really think it depends on how it is taught.

Tabitha pauses on the phone. She inhales and exhales slowly.

Well to be honest, I use it quite often as a bribe so 'if you put your heads down and do your work, we'll do some art later. I try and bring some of the academic side of it in when I do that, but quite often we've had a really busy day.

Teaching the arts has a lot to do with experience and knowledge of how to actually do it. I really just don't have either. I actually refuse to teach music. I hate teaching music. I won't do it if I can possibly get out of it. Whereas teaching visual arts, that's something I feel more comfortable in and can do. You know.

Tabitha stops midway through her sentence. *I wish I could see her in person rather than looking at the phone and trying to guess what is coming.*

I don't actually teach the arts here, but my relief teacher does ...

Besides, I'd consider myself more of a copier of the arts as opposed to a teacher. With sewing it's a lot of copying patterns or adjusting and changing patterns to come out how you want. I mean you can make it up entirely from scratch but it's not that good. I enjoy painting but I'm very, very bad at it and my idea of painting is to get an OHT[11] photocopy or copy other paintings or pictures that I like and project them onto a canvas and then copy them so it's more like a paint by numbers that I do.

The Importance of Monet

As part of the interview, I ask Tabitha to bring along an artefact that she could talk about over the phone. Tabitha had chosen a Monet print that she uses with her students. To Tabitha, it is important that she shows students other parts of the world beyond the rural community.

If I'm teaching a new concept, for example teaching water colours, I always try and make sure that I've got examples of that medium. I bring work [pictures] from my home that I've purchased over the years for the students to look at so they look at different forms of art. I find the pictures in books or

41

CHAPTER 3

on the Internet for them to have a look at. [They can] see this is what can be achieved using this medium if you practice it well enough.

I think that's important for kids to see these pictures. I want them to know that there is more to life than mustering. There is a world outside of this community. They don't get to go to big art galleries or museums and see a real Monet. So for me a poster of a Monet is better than nothing.

My parents wanted me out of my community, they wanted me to leave the property. They wanted me to leave – not be in the town that I'd grown up in. They wanted me as far away as possible that they could get me so that I could realise there were things other than this community. There were places and things to do and, and people to meet, other than those people that I'd grown up with. I think that's really important for kids and I think it's the same with anything that they learn in school, they need to learn that there's more than just mustering, there's more than just reading or writing, or doing their maths. There are things out there that maybe you won't have a chance to see such as a theatre performance in the city, but you need to know about it.

COMMUNITY STORY

Access to arts experiences in the region appears almost impossible. There are limited opportunities to view concerts, movies and theatre productions within the rural community. Occasionally, metropolitan arts groups travel to a town nearby.

I am intrigued. "So where would you go if you wanted to see a live performance?"

I think there is a town close by that might do something once a year or so. That's half an hour away. Otherwise, you need to go to Townsville. Townsville has concerts on occasionally – that's about four and a half, five hours away. Otherwise you hop on a plane and go to Brisbane or somewhere like that.

"Can you catch a plane directly from here though?"

Well there was a plane service from a town about an hour away. So you had to drive there and fly out but the rural plane company has gone bust. So being able to get a seat on the plane that the Government's organized at the moment is next to impossible. You just don't bother. You drive five hours to Townsville and get a plane there.

As I re-read about Tabitha's geographical location and isolation, I think about Costantoura's (2001) findings of the low amount of the arts that occurs outside of metropolitan areas. Living in a metropolitan area, I had easy access to any art form that I wanted to see.

42

AT THIS SCHOOL ARTS EDUCATION IS TRAVELLING ON A ROCKY ROAD

The Five Hour Drive for a Multi-School

Since there were limited opportunities for live performances, I was interested to know what arts activities the students experienced. Tabitha launches into an enthusiastic description of the planned multi-school.

We've actually got a multi-school this year. We had our first one last year. I ran a multi-school last year which was based around science and we had fourteen one teacher schools come in. So I think there were about 140, 150 kids plus the associated parents, teacher aides, adults, teachers, come in. We all had to go to [a bigger town] and we had a full week of science lessons. We're doing the same for the arts this year, so we've got a full week of performance based. Next year it will be visual arts so the kids will be learning visual arts, they'll be learning at a camp with about 140 other kids.

We're planning on doing it every second year from now on but it will be held in the same place. It's just a more central point for us and it's one of the bigger towns that we can find accommodation and a venue to hold it.

"So how do you get there?" I ask, puzzled by the location.

It's about five hours drive if the roads aren't too bad. We aren't one of the closest schools. There's some schools that are half an hour away, some schools that, my last school was two and a half three hours away. We've got five hours to go which is a bit more than some people. Having said that there are other schools that have got eight, nine, ten hours travel to get there.

I thought of the logistics of trying to organise excursions when I was a teacher. This was usually a fifteen minute bus trip into the city to the art gallery or a music concert. Tabitha's excursion was on a much, much larger scale. "How do you transport everyone there?" I ask.

It depends on the community and it depends on who gets in and gets the council bus. There's one council bus with ten seats, so even if I got the bus I couldn't take everybody. I could take the kids and me but I wouldn't be able to take my teacher aide and I wouldn't be able to take the parents that I need to take to help support it. So we'd need to have a second vehicle going anyway and that's a case of most of the schools. Some have access to either troop carriers or a bus of some sort, but they still need the parents to drive. Some schools don't have access to either of those so they just get the parents car pooling.

REFORM STORY

They're Putting Pressure on Us

Tabitha feels pressured in the teaching of arts education. She speaks of recent pressure from the Department to try and increase the arts in the Year

43

CHAPTER 3

of Creativity (2009). Tabitha has received emails and flyers about the year of creativity and encouraging the arts. She feels unsupported however, perhaps abandoned. While she knows it is important, she does not know how to teach the arts.

While the Education Department is saying visual arts are important, they're putting pressure on us and say[ing] 'you must do this and you must do that'. For a lot of the teachers because we haven't done that much on it [the arts] since uni[versity], and because so many years [since we had professional learning], it's just been that, you know the Friday afternoon bludge session they don't use it as well as it could be used.

Tabitha feels professional development in the arts is important to help increase her current arts knowledge. At the same time though, she expresses concern at the cost of professional development in rural areas. Tabitha says that professional development is *one of the things they're raising with the department actually,* referring to her learning community.

The cost of travel out here is very expensive. For example, for me to go to a principal's meeting which goes for four days, I'd have to leave the day before and I travel home on a weekend. It'll cost me in accommodation, food, travel and the cost of hiring a new teacher, well a teacher to cover me at the school while ...Close to three and a half, four thousand dollars. Now my grant budget for attending those meeting is a bit over three thousand dollars for the year and I have to go to four of those meetings each year. So I'm looking at shelling out close to $12,000 a year to go to the principal's meetings.

Then I have to look at the rest of the things around my school. I have water tanks that are broken, fences that are broken, very old resources – if I have any resources at all because the rats got in over the holidays and ate most of the things. So I need to look at what's best for me or what's best for the school. Do I spend the school budget on replacing those resources or fixing things around the school rather than going to professional development? I mean the cost for travel, the accommodation, even if I can get someone to replace me at the school makes it difficult. So you really, really need to pick very carefully what it is you go to.

"With the principal meetings, uhm, does the extra money come out of the school budget or out of your own pocket?" I ask.

Uhm a bit of both. Usually we factor in that it's gonna cost a lot more than the actual grant in full, so it comes out of that. A lot of us don't claim for things. If we're staying with friends, we're entitled to claim for accommodation. A lot of us don't do that ... most of us don't claim for food ...some people don't even claim for kilometres. So you know we can claim it back on tax, but

44

we certainly don't get as much back as we would if claiming it through the school. By not claiming it through the school we're not making people aware that there is such a problem ... but I mean ... Do we send our schools broke by claiming this stuff? So it's a bit of a catch-22 situation.

Everyone Should Just Shut Up

Tabitha spoke of the continual state and national policy reform. To Tabitha, this was seen as another barrier to her teaching of the arts. In the past two years, Tabitha had seen a move from outcomes based education to Essential Learning Statements within Queensland. Within this period she had also witnessed the introduction of:

- *Environmental Education for Sustainability* (2006)[12];
- *Smart Moves* (2007)[13];
- *Smart Classrooms* (2007)[14];
- *Literacy – The Key To Learning* (2006)[15]; *and*
- *NAPLAN*[16] (2008).

Continual policy reform continued to create pressure for Tabitha. As Tabitha spoke down the phone line, I could feel the stress increasing in her voice.

When I started teaching I had to learn all about the outcomes. Now when I first started my teacher training outcomes didn't exist, year two net didn't exist. Now I've started teaching I've had to learn about the year two net, I had to learn how to do outcomes. You know everybody just seems to get their head around it and then they say 'ohh we're going to essentials[17] this is what you've got to teach to now'. So, we've all spent the last two years struggling to integrate the essentials and learn how to use the essentials and now they're saying we're going for a national curriculum. Everybody should shut up – you need to pick something and stick to it for more than two years.

I'm a Teacher Not a Parent

Tabitha continues. Down the phone line, I can hear her voice becoming tense. She describes problems with overcrowded curriculums and not having enough time to teach existing subjects, especially the arts.

Keep it simple, primarily because we don't have the time to do everything they're saying to do. I think someone worked it out that we have something like ... I can't remember what the exact numbers [are], but say we have 1000 hours each year. We actually have something like over 1000 hours if you

CHAPTER 3

come down to it of what we need to be teaching. We don't have the time to teach what we're supposed to be teaching now. They keep saying things at us like 'Smart Moves' and then saying right, you've got to teach the virtues and you've got to teach this and you need to teach that. Your kids need to learn how to do this so you need to teach that. We don't have the time and it comes down to the fact that I'm a teacher I'm not a parent. If I wanted to be a parent I would have gone and had kids ...maybe that's something down the track, but it's certainly not where I'm at now.

I do object to teaching kids how to clean their teeth and that's something that I have had to have specific lessons in doing. The thirty minutes of sport each day, when I have kids who can't read, I'm not exactly 100 per cent keen on that. I try and integrate literacy where I can in, but that's really hard. I'd rather have them up here [in the classroom] doing an extra half an hour of reading or writing activities.

I think the policy makers need to realise that for everything that they add, everything that they tell us that we've got to do, they're going to have to start taking things out. And they're just not doing that, they're just keeping on adding things. They need to listen.

****

NOTES

[1] Sports Utility Vehicle
[2] Search Engine
[3] An Australian brand of beer
[4] A grill made up of wild animals and road kill
[5] The school identity has been kept anonymous
[6] Since the school does not have access to a visiting language teacher, all language classes are conducted over the internet and phone with a qualified teacher in a metropolitan area.
[7] Australian outback
[8] Region located in far north Queensland
[9] For privacy and protection, the name of the learning community has been withheld.
[10] Australian slang
[11] Overhead transparency
[12] (www.de-identified.com.au, accessed 15 March, 2009)
[13] (www.de-identified.com.au, accessed 15 March, 2009)
[14] (www.de-identified.com.au, accessed 15 March, 2009)
[15] (www.de-identified.com.au, accessed 15 March, 2009)
[16] National Assessment Program for Literacy and Numeracy www.naplan.edu.au, accessed 15 March, 2009)
[17] Essential Learning Statement (QSA, 2007)

CHAPTER 4

AT THIS SCHOOL ARTS EDUCATION IS PART OF THE HOLISTIC DEVELOPMENT OF ALL GIRLS

INTRODUCTION

The next chapter is another story constellation exploring the same topic of arts education as chapter three did. This time however there are two voices in the constellation. The intention is again to show the reader the importance of understanding the complexity of contexts. In this story constellation, the voice of the principal again stands beside that of the teacher. It is possible to see their individual values, beliefs and perspectives and how this appears within the educational landscape.

The school is the Maxwell Girls School. There is a year five teacher called Melissa Rafter and a principal called Christine Lynch. From the story constellation emerged three school values that ran as plotlines across the participants' stories: the holistic development of all students, the valuing of specialist teachers, and the importance of co-curricular activities. From school organisation, teachers knew their role within the school, especially in relation to the teaching of the arts.

The inquiry unfolded the values statement "at this school, arts education is part of the holistic development of all students". The statement captures the valuing of arts education within the school and the importance of arts involvement for all students. Strong teacher self-efficacy for the arts was evidenced in the capacity of Melissa to identify arts learning outcomes and to integrate the arts into her everyday teaching.

INTRODUCING THE MAXWELL GIRLS SCHOOLS

I am running late for my first appointment at the Maxwell Girls School. I had taken the wrong exit off the freeway and ended up lost in a sea of houses in the western suburbs of Brisbane. I open my old Brisbane 2003 Referdex[1] in the car and re-track my destination.

After finding the school's driveway and parking, I am greeted with the 'end of school day' bell. As I quickly walk through the front gate for the first

CHAPTER 4

time, I am drawn to the vibrant colours of blue and green for the student's free dress day. Girls are laughing, singing and playing. Usually the girls would be in a dark blue dress, black leather shoes and a blue blazer top. As I make my way to the reception, girls race past holding tennis racquets, hockey sticks and swimming goggles. The students are preparing for after school sport.

The Maxwell Girls School is an independent school that caters for girls from prep to year 12. It is located in an affluent suburb in Brisbane. I came to know the junior section of the school, where just over 300 girls from prep to year seven attended. The school prides itself on having a small school population, allowing a strong sense of community to develop between students, parents and teachers. Most classes within the junior school have between 20 and 25 students.

Generalist teachers at the Maxwell Girls School have access to many support staff. There is a full time teacher aide in prep and two other teacher aides who work alongside generalist teachers over the week. There are also library staff who play an active role in promoting reading within the school. The junior school has a full time music teacher and a full time visual arts teacher.

Girls attend weekly lessons in music and visual arts. During my first visit, I am blown away at how many instrument cases I see students carrying home. I later learn that instrumental lessons are part of the compulsory curriculum.

TEACHER STORY

Melissa Rafter is a third year beginning teacher in her late 20s. She invites me into her year five classroom after school for our interview. Upon entering the classroom, I am struck by all the visual arts projects on the walls. Bright colours are everywhere. The current Australian history unit has been aesthetically represented as flags, animals, landmarks and hands. An Australian map sits in the centre.

(Melissa's classroom displays, 2009)

SCHOOL ARTS EDUCATION IS PART OF THE HOLISTIC DEVELOPMENT OF ALL GIRLS

"Is it ok if we sit for the interview?" I ask.

"Sure, take a seat" she says. Melissa sits down at a group of four student wooden tables in the middle of the classroom. Underneath each desk are student tidy trays. I pull the chair out further from the desk. I know I will not fit under the child sized desk.

I take out the digital recorder and place it in the middle of the table. "Could you please tell me about your experiences with the arts, starting from your childhood". At the end of my last word I hit the record button. Melissa begins.

Growing Up in an Artistic Family

I grew up in a fairly artistic family I would imagine. My mother is a theatre lover. She grew up loving the arts and became a journalist and then transferred later on into being an English teacher and a drama teacher. Now, as a result of her love for the arts I suspect she instilled that in me, and so we attended lots of things along the way and performances here and there and all the musicals and all the plays and lots of arts exhibitions.

On the other side of the coin my dad was very interested in natural history and science, so we spent a lot of time in museums with him, so I got both sides of the coin. I think they influence me, because I went off to university and studied languages and tried a few different things, a little arts degree really, before deciding I'd give theatre a bit of a whirl.

So I did theatre at university[2] and then I had to translate that into some kind of a job because at that point I was feeling a little bit of the pressure, oh you know you're doing theater, you'll never get a job in that, which then, competitive person that I am, made me think yes I can and off I'll go and get one. So I worked for a Theatre Company[3] for a number of years there as the Executive Assistant for the Assistant Director Tom Brown[4], the General Manager and did a lot of casting work and reporting to the Board and lots of ins and outs, as those sort of roles really are, a lot of production work. And then I moved to Sydney and I did a similar role there which was great fun. I really loved being in the management side of the arts, behind the scenes. I was a stage manager at school. That was what I did while I was at high school, and so I wanted to apply that in a different way.

Having done all of that, while I was working in that area I did my education degree because I wanted to. Later on down the track I knew that being in the arts in that way was fine but I wanted to apply it to a broader scale, so teaching was a fabulous thing for me to do. But before I came to

CHAPTER 4

teaching I worked for three years in a Government role and I had a chance to see quite a lot of Australia and a lot of Queensland at all different levels of community and it was in that role really that it became apparent how important the arts in general are for communities, not necessarily going out to see performances or being part of plays, but it's just an important part of the rich fabric, I suspect of a community life. We went and visited the CWA[5], for example, and they'd have a local group doing bush poetry and that brought them so much joy, or we'd go to a country fair while I was with the Governor and we would be there looking at various patchwork examples. So I think it's an all pervading thing and the arts really for me are about entertainment and enjoyment and another way of expressing one's identity and one's culture.

I Was Lucky I Didn't Do the One Year Diploma

I think I was fortunate having done an undergraduate degree particularly in a performing arts area, like perhaps I had more exposure to that than some of my other colleagues who were studying at the time. Having said that though, we were very lucky, I didn't do the, one year post graduate diploma. I did a two year graduate diploma, so we had to do all of the subjects, rather than just a year fast track.

And as part of that degree there was a particular focus on arts education, so I did two, three subjects I think one on visual arts, one on performing arts, there was a music component.

I know though, having seen the young teachers coming through now, a couple of years after me, who are now being prac teachers[6] in my classroom – they're not necessarily getting that unless they particularly choose to do it. It seems now that it might be an elective or something that's an optional thing to be chosen rather than prescribed, you need to have experience in it though. The arts are really important. In this school, I use arts education as inbuilt into my integrated activities for literacy and numeracy and SOSE[7].

Re-Engaging with the Arts at a Personal Level

Knock, Knock, Knock.   Our interview is interrupted by a knock at the door. Melissa rises out of the student chair and walks to the doorway. There stands one of Melissa's students, looking for her musical instrument. The student has left it at school on the port rack and now can't find it. The teacher and student have a quick conversation of where the instrument could be.

50

(The year five classroom door, 2009)

Melissa returns a short time later to her chair in the middle of the classroom. *Sorry about that. School doesn't really end when the bell goes.* She laughs.

I again start the digital recorder, interested in her current experiences with the arts.

Her smile broadens. *Well, it has changed. I think because I saw and was so saturated by it for such a long period of time now it's purely enjoyment. I think it's interesting when you work as a professional in those areas and you are constantly surrounded by the work you have a different relationship to it when you're not necessarily being a professional in that area, so now it's an enjoyment factor. I choose the plays that I want to see, rather than go and see a production because we're looking at using it for something to fill a space or because we'd like to hire the director who's in such and such a thing to check out the work, so I'm really enjoying the stepping back process and being able to look at something and enjoy it for art sake rather than having your business hat on checking out someone's credentials perhaps.*

For Melissa, a re-engagement with the arts had occurred on a more personal level. She is no longer looking at the arts for another purpose (such as work). She can enjoy the arts for herself. *Pure bliss,* she smiles.

I Think I Facilitate Art

Melissa suggests she doesn't necessarily practice the arts (as an artist would) within the classroom, but she does facilitate the arts in most learning experiences.

I think I facilitate it. You know, the things that come from being an artistic person in the wake of others. I think I facilitate art more than an artist. I know I have, there are elements of what I do in, not necessarily in the classroom but also in volunteer work or, because I wear a number of other hats for

CHAPTER 4

different community organisations that I would say are artistic activities, but I don't think I practice art necessarily, no.

"So do you consider yourself a teacher of the arts?" I am intrigued.

Yeah absolutely. Melissa laughs. *I mean it doesn't have to be a great big long lesson, it might be reading a book and talking about you know Oodgeroo Noonuccal[8]. Who was she and why is she fantastic? Let's read a little bit of her poetry, let's go check it out you know, her five minute segue.*

Melissa pauses, before justifying her approach.

I think arts helps to round a person out. There are certain things, certain skills that come from studying an art form that don't necessarily come in other areas. There are great parallels between music, science and maths, for example about the way you think and the way you organise information. The same for theatre and drama, I think it's a really great way to bring out empathy and to teach social skills and it's a literacy tool as well, so I don't think you cannot have them. I think they're important for a curriculum, but I also think the curriculum is being less about silos and more about integration with pathways across all the areas.

"Could you elaborate on your approach a little more", I ask. Melissa's confidence in her knowledge begins to appear in her capacity to identify arts learning outcomes and arts integration.

Okay well you've got your maths, your science, your SOSE[9] and they're all subject areas and you timetable them all and instead of having them all timetabled I think they should be pathways to be able to use a creative element, say a musical element for your maths lesson, and be able to use an artistic mapping. You might be doing a mapping exercise, how can you use an artistic view point to help that geography lesson, so it's less about we're doing this now and we can only do those, and we can only use those skills and maths isn't just about adding all the numbers up, maths is also about thinking this way and thinking that way and, it's about thinking skills more than necessarily about subject areas I think.

Melissa's sense of confidence became further evidenced as she starts to describe the importance of arts thinking skills. She believes these skills can be *carried over* and are important for other subject areas.

Thinking, organisation, expression, thinking laterally, thinking outside the box, other things too about being able to take on someone else's point of view. That's really important too and to see things from perhaps a different angle, looking for the things that are missing, that's a really important thinking skill, it's not about the stuff that's on the page, what's not being said, that's really important too, so what's the author not saying or what isn't being you know and being able to, the social skills, you know a lot of kids when you see

52

SCHOOL ARTS EDUCATION IS PART OF THE HOLISTIC DEVELOPMENT OF ALL GIRLS

a play or when you do a drama activity with a group of children they pick up on the finer points, the subtleties about how humans communicate with body language and tone. Those things you don't necessarily get from another medium, as well or as effectively.

My Ideal School Day Is Here

Melissa describes the school day at the Maxwell Girls School as *hectic, busy* and *intense*. While each day is different, she recounts the day that has just unfolded in her year five classroom.

Okay today. What did we do today? Wednesday, okay, we arrived, I'm just looking at the timetable over there to remember what we did. That's terrible. Melissa lets out a big laugh. *A Brain freeze. I'll have to grab my other plan.* She jumps out of her seat and returns with her teaching diary.

What did we do? She looks down her page. *Oh we had a test first up, there you go. Standards of accountability right there, for the end of our unit. A SOSE test on Aboriginal and Australian history. It was exciting stuff,* Melissa states sincerely.

And then we watched a little bit of a film on Captain Cook[10], the girls went to music, and at the moment they're all in year five bands, so they had their instruments with them today and they broke up into their instrument groups. Melissa smiles. Which is going well for some and not so good for others, but they're getting there.

Then they came back from morning tea and they had LOTE[11], and that LOTE lesson today was, the Japanese girls acted it out, they did some dressing up in Kimonos and acting out the difficulties of what it means to be wearing those clothes and how hard it would have been to do every day active tasks, and the German girls were learning a song. Then we did maths activities. We had a measuring outdoors maths activity. We had to work out how many cars there were and we graphed them. Some girls were on the computer doing some stuff with Smart Kiddies in an interactive website and we had a couple of girls who were doing brain games on the floor, building stuff, other girls who were doing a number facts race and the last group of girls were doing a piece of art, measuring how long didgeridoos are, and then creating their own for a measurement task.

Then we did some visualisation and some imaginary skills, it's called Scamper. The girls lie on the carpet, they have to close their eyes and I run them through an imaginary activity and they have to think outside of the box in order to do some visualisation, which is good fun. After lunch we had some reflection time. They each have a diary and they sit down and they can

53

CHAPTER 4

express themselves however they'd like to in that diary. I don't read them unless they'd like me to read them, just as a way, gives them some down time and to create to think about what they've been doing. We did some English rotations this afternoon, some reading groups. The girls were doing ... Melissa lets out a sigh ... *I'm just trying to think what I did with some comprehension. There was a group doing poetry. They had to take their poem outside and to interview each other as if they were, some skits I suppose in the interviews, and then we did a class reading of our novel, which was exciting, and then we went home. Woohoo!* Melissa again laughs out loud ... *the girls are off to sport. They're not always that big, but today was a big day.*

Melissa' school day does not end here. After my interview, she tutors older students in French, before going to professional association meetings for the night. I wonder how she has so much energy to keep going. I also start to wonder about beginning teacher burnout.

I continue with our interview. "So what would your ideal school day be like?"

Ideal school day. Melissa pauses as she appears to gather her thoughts. *I like our school days here. I think we have the balance right between all the subjects. I think we're lucky in that we're able to. We've got a very supportive leadership team, there's room to try new things, there's scope to try new, different technologies and ideas and because it's a small school as well there's a lot of opportunity to do things with the older and the younger levels. So the year 5s, we often go up to the year 11 and 12s and we'll do some activities with them. If it's science we might be in the labs, they might teach us the concept sort of stuff, if it's little girls we might do buddy reading or friendship groups or finger paintings or Easter activities or stuff, so I think that's pretty useful.*

I inject. "You use a lot of arts. A lot of teachers don't actually do that".

Really, oh but it's great fun and the girls love it and it keeps them, it keeps them motivated. I don't do it for everything, most of them I've had, you know maths groups, for example they had four tasks to do and that was one of them and the other you know, but it just adds an extra dimension, the pictures of the things they're doing, and it makes them apply their knowledge in a different way. Learning for life.

PRINCIPAL STORY

Christine Lynch is the principal of the junior school at Maxwell Girls School. I had made an appointment to interview her in her office after school. The time is now 3.10pm and I am sitting quietly in reception.

SCHOOL ARTS EDUCATION IS PART OF THE HOLISTIC DEVELOPMENT OF ALL GIRLS

I wait on the comfy leather chair. Around me are certificates and trophies that dominate the shelves and walls. I pick up the 'glossy' school prospectus and have a quick flick, admiring all the happy, smiling girls in the photos. The photos show a strong sense of community, with younger students often photographed with older students. All students appear friendly, happy and engaged in learning.

On the wall hangs whole school portraits. At the top of the portrait is a banner of the school's name, emblem and Latin motto. Down the bottom appears the year. School photos are taken every second year.

I pick up the newsletter and read about student success in sports, arts and academic pursuits. In the photos, it appears that students are rewarded with new embroidery on their blazer pockets. I further read about past students who have achieved great feats since leaving school. My mind starts to wonder. Were all independent girls schools similar? Were rewards shown on blazer pockets? Did schools still advertise the success of past students?

I again glance around the reception. The reception is identical to the one I had known as a teenager. The trophy cabinet smells of fresh varnish. Glossy school newsletters and magazines are the only reading material. A CD of the school choir plays in the background. I reflect back to my own experiences at an all girls boarding school. I remember lining up for the school photo that would take at least an hour to organize. It was usually held during an English lesson when we were rehearsing our monologues from Shakespeare.

I reflect on the school images I had experienced as a student. Girls were always well groomed, with stockings, long skirts and hats. Smiles, engagement in learning and the community dominated every shot. From looking around the reception, the memories come rushing back.

The receptionist draws me back into the present. "The principal will now see you Susanne".

Christine Lynch greets me at the door with a big smile. She is an older women, probably mid 50s with a gentle voice. I follow her down the corridor and into her office. *"Have you been for a tour of the school?"* she asks.

"Not yet," I respond.

Well let me show you this wonderful school. She turns around and I follow her out of reception.

Christine starts her tour of the junior school. There are only a few buildings. The majority of school infrastructure resides in the secondary school across the road. Sport facilities include: tennis courts, 25 metre pool, a fitness centre and sixteen acres of sporting fields. Arts facilities include: art gallery, dance studio music practice rooms and a performing arts complex with a

CHAPTER 4

200 seat auditorium. Academic facilities are also extensive. They include: the Science and Technology centre, five computer rooms (one of which is a Robotics laboratory and another for Languages Other Than English) laptops located in most classrooms (a total of 345 computers for student use); an air-conditioned library and a chapel.

As we walk, Christine talks openly with her primary students. The girls run up to her, keen to share what they had learned for the day. Christine's memory is impressive. She knows something about every child's hobbies and interests. The caring community at Maxwell Girls School begins to shine through in the relationship between principal and student.

Christine speaks highly of the year five teacher, Melissa Rafter. According to Christine, *Melissa is a fantastic teacher who was often involved in different types of learning experiences to cater for the students' needs. You could see her dedication to the year five girls. She also tutored older girls in French.*

I Don't Really Feel Comfortable Teaching the Arts

We return to Christine's air-conditioned office to begin the interview. I place the digital recorder on her desk amongst all the paper work. Christine begins with her personal history of teaching and her feelings of incompetence when trying to teach the arts.

When I first started teaching I had to teach both music and art, visual arts and felt a complete failure, because, even though I was a lover of music and I had some skills at piano playing I really was not able to teach music. I felt inadequate and those feelings of inadequacy certainly went with all the artistic visual arts that were necessary in those days.

I mean I don't really consider myself an artist. I play the piano badly and I enjoy photography, but you know I don't think that you would describe me as an artist. Christine laughs. *I have a son and I have just seen how wonderful music has been for him and his friends. It has really shaped who he is and taught him very vital life skills. You notice that all the students who do music and the arts are the students who receive awards at speech day.*

This is the problem with the arts not being academic though. I think at the level in the primary school there's not a lot of rigor in it. Now that my music teachers would argue against that because and ... I think this particular primary school has an advantage of having specialist teachers both in art from about year four upwards all the way through of course for music. We don't have dance or any kind of media studies. So we have the advantage for having two specialist teachers, now ... that puts more academic rigor into it

56

as compared to lots of other schools because this is a very specialist area. Not anybody can teach music you know. I mean I can teach art but I could not be considered in any way any kind of artist and ... sorry I forgotten where I was going with that one.

Christine and I share in laughter. We acknowledge each other with a smile.

I continue where the conversation has ended. "It's an interesting idea this that whether there should be specialists who deal with the arts subjects or if it should be pushed more back on to the generalist teacher".

Well I ... I feel very strongly that it's a specialist subject and to do it justice you cannot make it an academic subject unless you've got specialists doing it. They bring the rigor and understanding that many generalists[12] just don't have.

SCHOOL STORY

On another tour around the school with Christine, I notice amazing artworks that appear in the classrooms and stairwells. A colourful mosaic catches my eye. It consists of self-portraits of all the junior school community smiling. Everybody is there on the wall, staff and students. Christine tells me it was created as a permanent memory of students in the school around 2004. She proudly shows me her self-portrait within the mosaic. I feel slightly confused. While she does not feel confident teaching the arts, she had created a mosaic of herself.

(Mosaic, 2009)

Oh that was part of the community activity we did. It wasn't competitive at all. Everyone enjoyed taking part, staff and students. We came up with a mosaic of the entire school. I immediately think of the united school community that was emerging. art works fill the buildings, exemplifying this notion.

CHAPTER 4

School Values 1: Specialist Teachers Are Vital to this School

As Christine tells me her story about the school, she reveals an important school value. According to Christine, all teachers at the Maxwell Girls School are in a privileged position. *We're privileged because we have access to specialist teachers. It allows the school to give students a balanced education. The arts are such a specialised area and require specialist teachers.*

Melissa also mentions this *position of privilege.* She has *access to quality specialist teachers for music and the arts, and generalist teachers who try to integrate the arts into all other learning areas.* Melissa suggests that *all teachers know their role* and this was one of the reasons the school functioned so well in the arts.

Melissa continues to explain teacher roles. *There should be a clear definition about the roles and how education should be framed ... I think if it's black and white and separated then that's fabulous because neither has to interfere with the other and they can be completely separate programs which works well when you've got individuals who try and do what they need to do ... So if you're a classroom teacher you can use the arts in these ways to support what you're doing or you can have a focus on a thing in a particular term and have a more detailed in-depth unit. But then the specialist teachers have their own particular niche and they're looking at doing this and it's more skills based and it needs that, so that classroom teachers don't feel that they have to be specialist teachers and specialist teacher know what their role is, and it might be supported by the classroom teacher in an ideal world ... But in schools who don't have the specialist teacher it becomes difficult.*

See at this school, we're just so lucky to have what we have. I think it works wells and I like our system the way it is. So I think we're doing a really good job in supporting that. But for schools that don't have that option, they have to really decide what's important to their school. I think it would be a shame if arts education dropped off ... It seems that there are lots of generalist teachers but there aren't any specialist teachers. Those people [specialist teachers] are worth their weight in gold and they need to find a way to keep them. The specialist teachers here are brilliant.

School Values 2: the School's Focus on Holistic Development

The driving force behind the high arts exposure within Maxwell's Girls School appears to be a strong focus on holistic development. Christine suggests the school *is very conscious of Howard Gardener's multiple intelligences.* She thinks *it is one thing to have a high IQ*[13] *but intelligence goes way beyond*

58

SCHOOL ARTS EDUCATION IS PART OF THE HOLISTIC DEVELOPMENT OF ALL GIRLS

that. And pursuing your talents and skills in dance or music or visual arts is equally as important as it is through word or numbers. Creativity is part of the musical intelligence.

Christine smiles. She gathers her thoughts before explaining the second value. *At times here at this school they do try to create assessment opportunities for children so that they can express themselves in those different ways. But even if you take away the assessment aspect to be able to express anything in different ways ... using all those multiple intelligences is important.*

We're educating children for life and this is a very important part of life and it could be an ongoing joy to people for the future even if they don't choose it as their occupation they can get enjoyment from appreciating music or playing a musical instrument or going to the theatre or ... you know doing photography.

The school's holistic development focus is evidenced in Melissa's teaching philosophy of using the arts as a learning style, *to cater for the learning needs of students.* She echoes educational values I have just heard from the principal. *I mean I know that sounds very fluffy, but when you actually do it, it really helps them to engage and be interested in what they're doing. So if it's a drama thing they'll go and create a play about it. If it's a music thing, they'll write a song. If it's athletics and hands on they might create some kind of sporting game.*

Learning Here Is Not Just about Literacy and Numeracy

Most schools nowadays place a huge focus on literacy and numeracy. We don't do that here. We believe in the holistic development of children. Christine leans back in her chair and smiles.

"So what do you mean by literacy, numeracy and the arts", I ask.

I see literacy as the ability to effectively communicate both in reading, writing and orally. Numeracy would have to be the ability to use numbers to calculate and to solve mathematical problems. Finally, the arts is the ability to express artistic and creative skills and knowledge and these would be expressed via music, visual arts, dance, drama and media.

The definitions just mentioned by Christine are similar to the definitions I had heard from Melissa in a previous interview. Melissa has suggested that *literacy is the ability to communicate clearly across a wide range of mediums. Numeracy is being able to use numbers in a nut shell, effectively in everyday situations. The arts provide an opportunity for creative self expression.* Both show clear links to the valuing and importance of each subject, with all subjects equal in the curriculum.

59

CHAPTER 4

Melissa says that parents in the school were supportive of the holistic approach and the valuing of the arts. *I think that parents generally are shifting now to understand, maybe it would have been more tricky five years ago, but I think now parents are starting to understand that learning is different from learning when they were at school and it's not about the rigid desks. And just because it doesn't look like that doesn't mean it's not having the same effect.*

I mean all the teachers do it here. It is a school that tries to encompass the different ways that girls learn. I love using the arts as a learning style. I picked up a lot by being around a number of teachers in this school. We're really good at doing that.

Melissa smiles. *Look if it's boring for me, it's probably going to be boring to them. I know that learning isn't always fun. There are some bits that are hard and dry and some bits that you just have to teach in a pretty pragmatic way. I think it doesn't always have to be like that.*

School Values 3: Co-curricular Activities Provide Opportunities for Girls to Succeed

The principal begins to describe numerous co-curricular activities for the primary school girls. At the Maxwell Girls School, co-curricular activities have their own section on the school website (www.de-identified.com.au, accessed 20 April, 2009)[14]. They are considered an important part of student development.

Well we have private music lessons and those take place in school time in most cases ... We have an art club which runs two or three afternoons a week. The art specialist runs that after school and I think that involves children from ... I think year three to seven are invited ... We have some musicians, but I don't know if you'd call this extra curricular or co-curricular but we have concert bands and stage bands and groups like that within the school. Some of those we have are just junior school groups, but also some of our better junior school children play in the senior school.

The principal takes a breath and continues.

Now those girls then could be involved in things like the school musical which is run usually every year, although I don't think there is going to be one this year for the first year for a long time and that's usually with an all boys school. So our younger girls can be exposed to that sort of thing ...

Christine pauses, before reflecting on the actual class music program.

Within our music program, we have a year four strings group. Now that is within the curriculum, so every girl in year four is taught how to play the violin ... and then in year six we have percussion and brass classes, so all of

60

SCHOOL ARTS EDUCATION IS PART OF THE HOLISTIC DEVELOPMENT OF ALL GIRLS

the girls they've either percussionists or in the brass section and then they have the opportunity to all perform together ... they're taught separately and then brought together as a big year six group.

Melissa shares similar beliefs about the importance of the music program. She discusses the skills building progression that is built into learning at the junior and senior level.

Our girls are introduced in year five to their brass instrument or whatever it might be. By the time they get to year 7, they have the opportunity to be part of a larger, whole school senior concert band. So a student in year 7 could be sitting next to a year 12 student who is a highly skilled musician by that point, and they can grow in that way. I think that really fosters the confidence of that child to see if they can get to be as good as the person next to them ... And I think we try to have some real outcomes for those performance groups, so they have performances that they are working towards and the junior girls see that. We've got a dance club for example in year 4 and it's a lunchtime dance club. Those year 4's see that when they join the senior school they can be part of the stage group and the stage group are more of a professional dance club and they do things and they win awards and they go off to all of the Eisteddfods. So there's a planned approach from a junior level to a senior level and how those things might fit together to give them an experience, rather than just being a one off.

It is assumed that involvement in co-curricular programs will lead girls to develop discipline and determination, *considered valuable components of personal development.* In the secondary school, girls are encouraged into many co-curricular activities.

The focus on co-curricular activities at the junior school level appears to resonate from the senior school. Melissa considers working at a prep to year 12 school as *fantastic*, with the opportunity to work together and share facilities and resources.

Having a prep to year 12 school means we have access to resources that perhaps may not be available in an everyday primary school. We have access to bigger drama spaces, we've got a bigger IT[15] department who can help us with film projects and we've got a bigger music staff that run larger ensembles.

COMMUNITY STORY

Connecting with the community is highly valued by Christine and Melissa. In separate interviews, both mention the importance of arts activities for connecting the school with the community.

CHAPTER 4

I sit in the cool of Christine's office as she begins. She explains that the arts groups function as a showcase for the children's abilities. Christine describes an example of girls visiting and performing at a retirement village close to the school. *Well it certainly happens on an annual basis. We have what we call an arts and music evening usually in about third term and that is done with a visual display. We sort of, you know, have wine and cheese and have a look at all the children's artwork and then we move out and have the concert. The exact program is replicated the next day and we usually invite local community groups in the morning. They have a chance to look at the artwork and then we sort of repeat the concert.*

We also have similar situations. For instance last year, a year three and four choir at Christmas time walked to the local retirement village up the top of the hill and put on a performance for those people up there.

As I sit in the comfy chair listening to Christine, my mind creates questions. I am intrigued to know if visiting arts organisations and artists also visited the school.

Christine nods. *We've had artists in residence in the senior school but not here. In the past we've had Arts Council presentations and things like that. We also go to excursions, places like the Art Gallery in town. Last year the girls worked with the Art Gallery when the Andy Warhol exhibit was here. I know a number of our teachers took children in to see that display and that translated into work in the classroom.*

When I talk to Melissa about community involvement, she shares similar stories about the community. She describes an upcoming experience of a visiting author.

Next term we have an author coming. Jane Davis. Our novel study for the term is a book about the stolen generation. She's fantastic. She's just fabulous. She comes in and runs it, not 'hey this is my book isn't it great'. She runs writing workshops around the book for the day so that's really groovy.

Melissa pauses, before remembering about an artist who is coming into her classroom next week. *Actually next week, we've got an indigenous person, Rick Rosser. He comes in and does craft and arts activities. So we're doing face painting and ochre and fire sticks and black stuff. We really try and integrate with whatever our base theme is. Involving people from the community is really important.*

REFORM STORY

Christine discusses current educational reforms that are occurring. She stresses that as an independent school, they *can avoid some of the pressures*

SCHOOL ARTS EDUCATION IS PART OF THE HOLISTIC DEVELOPMENT OF ALL GIRLS

from school reform. She feels *lucky to be at this school as opposed to a state school.* She smiles. *Here, the school can decide where emphasis is placed in the curriculum.*

Melissa suggests similar feelings associated with working at an independent school. While she knows *the policies are from the state and federal governments,* she is *more interested in the school's policies as opposed to state policies.* Melissa describes being lucky to be in a supportive school that can generally choose what they do.

I ask Melissa if she ever feels pressure in her teaching.

Melissa wiggles in her chair. She inhales slowly. *Absolutely, yep, and not just governments, parents, the general community, you know consistent pressure. Everyone's got an idea on what makes a good education and what is not good educational practice.* Melissa suggests that pressure would always be part of her teaching and would increase with greater accountability.

I am interested to see Christine's and Melissa's views on the current focus on literacy and numeracy reform. Christine immediately raises concern for the teaching of the arts. Before I finish the question, her words are racing.

I do think the federal government's push at the moment to elevate English, maths, science and history is going to make a very interesting situation for subjects in the arts. If you are going to spend all of your time, and we don't know what time allocations are yet, but if those were going to be the compulsory subject set, it could mean that there will be a push in only those areas – we just won't be able to fit anything else in.

Christine suggests that the arts need to be elevated within the school. The current government *did not see it as important as it perhaps should be.*

I mean, it's a little difficult from a primary school perspective … I guess the governments have got to put money into the arts in the community, because there is not much point, particularly if someone wants to go through school and become an artist or a musician, unless there is somewhere for these people to go as a career path. There is very, very limited career paths in those occupations.

The government needs to start at the end

Christine glances sideways. The hum of the air-conditioner fills the silence. She breathes in slowly before continuing.

I think governments need to start at the end, creating the jobs and then giving some idea that there is a career path involved in that. I know from a primary school perspective we're not worried about what you're going to do when you leave school. But I think it would change people's and society's perspective of the importance of the arts. I think that at a primary school level,

CHAPTER 4

parents feel that it's a nice little thing for their daughter to be able to play the piano or to do a bit of ballet. It's just, it's very much more than a hobby.

****

Melissa does not feel comfortable with the NAPLAN[16] tests. She describes reports that have emerged in local newspapers of schools practicing exclusively for the test. *Entire days of practice.* She sits upright in her chair and clenches her fist. Melissa suggests that this type of testing is not an effective way of learning for students. *Ridiculous.*

I think practicing for a test is not an effective way of learning ... I think NAPLAN is a response to accountability issues in schools and making governments feel like they've got something down on paper and they can say this is how everything is going. I think kids are severely disadvantaged if they have to spend their time doing reams and reams of practice tests because it's not engaging them at all and they're not really learning.

Look, I'll show you the sorts of stuff that we do for NAPLAN. Melissa walks to the smart board and turns it on from the laptop.

"You're very lucky to have a smart board" I say, thinking of the schools I had visited in the last week that did not.

Melissa laughs. *I love it. I would never not have one. Whatever school I go to next, assuming I'm in school, it would have to have a smart board.*

She clicks to a practice question her students have been answering. Melissa had created the question herself. It was a mathematical question, with the answer and a division sign. The numbers to compute the answer were missing. *I think this is more effective because they have to think differently. It's actually stretching their thinking skills, which is really what they should be doing anyway. It's terrible. Yes there are going to be parents who say why hasn't my child done this, that or the other but it's not just about the year five teacher or the year three teacher or the year nine or the year seven teacher, it's about all the school they've had up until that point and I think that's where the argument is getting waylaid. It is impossible and unfair for that teacher to take the weight of the shoulder for all the other years. It's a process, it's not about one person.*

She switches off the smart board and sits back in the chair. She continues discussing her dislike of standardised testing. *Well you know high stakes testing, I think it is a reaction to a government issue. I don't think it is a true application of how kids learn. You know some of the questions that are asked, are asked in such a way that they are not actually testing the child's numeracy skills. It's testing whether or not the child can read the question.*

64

SCHOOL ARTS EDUCATION IS PART OF THE HOLISTIC DEVELOPMENT OF ALL GIRLS

Does the child understand the question? It's not whether or not they can add. Same for the grammar questions. There's actually not been a study that links a child's ability to find a noun in a sentence and whether or not they're a literate person. There's no correlation between the two so why test it?

Where Are the Professional Development Opportunities in the Arts?

Christine admits that she *can't remember anything being offered* for arts professional development for generalist teachers. Melissa has seen a few opportunities for teacher professional development however this is through involvement in professional organisations such as the English Teachers Association. Occasional workshops are run for drama activities, however these are not suitable for primary classrooms.

Melissa suggests that professional development in the arts would actually be difficult to organise, as teachers would all have different skill levels. According to Melissa, *generalist teachers have either had or not had experiences with music and the arts themselves. It is a specialised and skilled area. You either know what you're doing or you don't. You know you can either play the keyboard and use it as part of the classroom or you don't do it. It may be more tricky for some arts than others.*

Melissa taps the pen from the smart board on the desk, before talking about the professional learning that generalist teachers need.

It's a bit scary I think for teachers who've been there for a long time, when people come and say hey there's this great thing you've got to be doing it and you need to do it now, get into it. There needs to be a developed approach. For example, here's some simple ideas and really simple 5 minute stuff that you can do that are practical and easy that won't take you 3 hours to read the handbook or the document because if that happens and it just gets put on the shelf and it never happens anyway, so it's just those really simple small ideas that are the ones I think that are a lot more likely to be taken up. I'm doing this, it's working really well, let me share it, could be done through some kind of an online forum or a you know a professional level website for teachers that allows them to share things that are working. I think keep it simple.

****

NOTES

[1] Brisbane street map
[2] University has been de-identified

CHAPTER 4

[3] The Theatre Company has been de-identified
[4] Pseudonym
[5] Country Women's Association
[6] Pre-service teachers on school experience
[7] Studies of Society and Environment
[8] An Australian poet, political activist, artist and educator. Oodgeroo Noonuccal was the first Aboriginal woman to publish a book of verse.
[9] Studies of Society and Environment
[10] Famous explorer of Australia
[11] Language Other Than English
[12] Generalist Teacher
[13] Intelligence quotient
[14] The school identity has been kept anonymous.
[15] Information Technology
[16] National Assessment Program for Literacy and Numeracy

CHAPTER 5

ASSESSMENT IS A HOLISTIC JUDGEMENT

Do I Want This Pre-Service Teacher Teaching My Children?

INTRODUCTION

This constellation examines the shared lived experience of a practice triad in a small kindergarten in Brisbane Australia. The practice triad consists of Simone Smith, the kindergarten teacher with over 30 years experience, Talia Brown a recently graduated early childhood teacher who was supervised by Simone, and Megan Miles, a university teacher educator who supervised the professional experience. The story constellation explores assessment during professional experience against the backdrop of changing agendas and requirements for early childhood education. It also probes the similarities and differences in perceptions between the key actors on the quality of the professional experience.

INTRODUCING THE KINDERGARTEN

The Hapvale Community Kindergarten is located in a large city centre in South-East Queensland. It is next door to a large shopping centre, followed by a collection of car yards. Children come to the kindergarten from all across the local suburb. It is a non-profit organisation, whose income is derived from Government subsidies and fees charged to parents.

The kindergarten has been running for over 30 years and was designed to allow ample space for children to play. The kindergarten consists of an outside natural play space that includes a digging patch and an open air amphtitheatre. The playground facilities are designed to foster gross motor development. Inside, there is an open space filled with shelves, desks and mat space. Inside there is also a wide range of resources that are designed to develop children's play and learning.

Over the course of the week there are two groups of 20 children (turning four years of age by 30th June). Children attend the kindergarten five days over a fortnight. Each group has a university qualified teacher and a teaching

67

CHAPTER 5

assistant. Children bring their own lunch. Operating hours are usually 9am to 2.30pm Monday to Friday.

The Kindergarten is guided by the Early Years Learning Framework for Australia (DEEWR, 2009) and the Queensland Kindergarten Learning Guideline (QSA, 2010). The website states that the Community Kindergarten will (2012):

1. Challenge and support each child to maximise their potential for learning by responding to their individual needs and capabilities, family and cultural backgrounds, interests and learning styles.
2. Provide a learning environment that engages children in learning, is aesthetically pleasing, is safe and hygienic and is environmentally sustainable.
3. Engage parents as partners though: shared commitment to children's learning through discussion, collaboration and documentation; participating in learning experiences with children at the kindergarten; decision making about centre policy through discussions and representation on the management committee; show support and respect for parenting practices through discussion, information and participation; and preparation of children for transitions to school.
4. Provide safe and collaborative working environments for staff through: a shared commitment to high quality early childhood education; respect for professional knowledge and skills of each staff member; an environment of collaboration and support; and practices that protect the health, safety and wellbeing of staff.

I am immediately drawn to point four about the collaborative working environment for staff. I wonder if this philosophy also extends to pre-service teachers.

When I visit the kindergarten, I walk through the tall gate and along the path. It reminds me of the kindergarten I attended. Not much seemed to have changed from what I remembered as a child.

Inside there are different corners for different activities. There is a corner for blocks, dress up clothes, cushions, painting, science, patterns music and art. In the middle of the room is a big carpet for children to sit around. To the side of the big open classroom is a bathroom hidden behind glass windows. The toilets and hand basins are of children's size.

SUPERVISING TEACHER STORY

I interview Simone in a local coffee shop on a busy Tuesday morning near the kindergarten. Customers are watching the Olympics on the flat screen TV, wondering if Australia will win a gold medal. The lunch time crowd begins to enter and I try and find a quiet corner for us to conduct our interview.

Simone is running late after helping out educators in Family Day Care. She is being paid to help train staff about new early childhood requirements. I order a coffee and set up my notes. She quickly enters, orders an espresso and sits down on the padded chair.

Simone Smith has been a kindergarten teacher for over 30 years. She started teaching in 1978 in a rural community kindergarten, then came to her current kindergarten. She worked full time there until 1987, before switching to part time work. She is a qualified early childhood teacher and is currently completing a Master of Early Childhood Education.

Simone is passionate about young children and had a particular interest for early childhood music. She works five days a fortnight and is on the executive committee of an early childhood teacher professional organisation. The early childhood organisation is dedicated to professional development and learning of early childhood teachers.

Barriers to Supervision

Simone has previously supervised 20 pre-service teachers from the local universities. Simone comments that until recently, they would take a student each year. She supervised her last student, Talia Brown in 2010. Since then Simone has been too busy to supervise university pre-service teachers. She says the current changes in early childhood education and care in Australia has intensified her workload. In particular, she notes that the new external assessments by the Federal Government has increased her workload. She notes that the increase in paperwork has been created by having to continuously write around the standards.

I haven't had any students for a while as I don't feel I could do both the student and my job justice. With the extra work involved with the new curriculum, assessment by the Office for Early Childhood Education and Care and the development of the centre's quality improvement plan I didn't feel I would have enough time at the end of each day to spend with a student. I am working till 5 and 6pm several nights a week at the kindergarten and then going home and doing another 10 hours a week on average on computer filing and documentation for 20 children.

I ask Simone about the other barriers to supervising pre-service teachers. Her espresso arrives at the same time. She takes a sip and reflects.

Time, time time. You need between 30 and 45 mins each day to give feedback and help prepare student for the next day. Also it takes time at home

CHAPTER 5

*for the teacher to go through preservice teachers work and provide feedback.
They need a mentor and it takes a lot of time. It takes time for continual
assessment and feedback.*

She pauses.

*Actually, the way that experienced teachers plan is quite different to how
preservice teachers need to plan. Experienced teachers are usually only
noting things that are new/different/need immediate attention or follow
up, so preservice teachers may not gain much from looking at a teacher's
planning. It is hard to share with students sometimes as it is a type of hidden
knowledge. You have to make this knowledge explicit and then assess it with
the student. Also in the past many kindergarten teachers were doing very
limited planning and didn't show students. Not sure what happens now,
but I assume no-one gets away with no planning so perhaps more sharing
is occurring. I shared all our planning with Talia. She was a really good
student.*

"And have you ever had any negative experiences with pre-service
teachers?" I ask.

Simone nods.

"So how did you deal with the pre-service teacher during assessment?" I
am intrigued.

*Similar to dealing with difficult parents, trying to see their point of view,
clearly articulating responsibilities, framing it up as a 'learning experience'.
We did have a student who was very difficult one year, and it put us off
students for a few years. We just decided not to take anymore until we had
recovered from all the stress. I have friends who will never take a student
again.*

I pause. "What was the role of the university supervisor?"

Simone pauses and looks into her coffee. *We rarely saw a university
supervisor. Usually they are just available to contact by email or phone,
so really not much help. Other colleagues have mentioned times when
they were very concerned about the preservice teacher and were told that
they had to get the student through. This can be particularly challenging
when you have a student [pre-service teacher] whose English is a Second
Language.*

*Another issue about visits is that kindergarten teaching is very busy
and there is no-one who can teach so that you can take a break to talk to
visitors. It is almost impossible to have a complex and detailed discussion
when you are trying to teach a group of three to four year olds at the same
time. I can't talk to the university supervisor when I am responsible for the
children.*

ASSESSMENT IS A HOLISTIC JUDGEMENT

DUELLING ROLES EXIST

Simone continues to talk about the role of the supervising pre-service teachers. She continues to talk about her situation as common for all early childhood teachers.

The skills for teaching kindergarten children are quite different from mentoring and assessing student teachers – it is a different kind of relationship- long term with children and short-term with the student. Not everyone feels confident about doing it and because they are supposed to be an expert, particularly if they are already feeling a little unsure about their own teaching practice. It is a different skill-set to assess children and pre-service teachers.

I nod, remembering the experiences with my first pre-service teacher as a supervisor. "Do you ever feel a conflict of roles?" I ask.

Yes, sometimes the assessing is difficult particularly when you can see that the student has tried but still isn't up to the standard they need to be. Yes definitely an issue. It is all good if you have a competent and enthusiastic student because there is enough positive feedback to balance any "constructive criticism". Also I suspect teachers have difficulty providing feedback that is not positive because of the "only say nice things at kindy" culture. Kindergarten teachers are kind and nice people. They don't like to say negative things.

"So it is difficult for a kindergarten teacher to provide criticism?" I am intrigued.

It can be really difficult. We always want to work with children and know that they will develop when they are ready. We aren't used to evaluating adults in a different mind-set. We don't evaluate children the same way.

I pause. "What do you think about the assessment role you are given and associated paperwork?"

It can be difficult when you only have the student for a few days e,g, if you are in a shared position such as part time- you may only have that student for four days on a ten day practicum. How can I assess them on their entire performance? I act as a type of gate keeper to the profession and I make judgements with limited knowledge about the student.

Simone makes direct eye contact and breathes.

Also, I am not sure that teachers, let alone the students, always understand what is being assessed. Teachers do not always read the handbook, or they do read it but in the context of what they think should be happening. I have often heard of teachers who are expecting students to do full group teaching when the university professional experience handbook has said only observation.

CHAPTER 5

"And how do you find the university professional experience handbook?"

Simone laughs. *Some are better than others. If they are too long no-one reads them. I think it would be better for a university-based person to come out to a local venue) and meet with teachers and perhaps also preservice teachers to talk about expectations, benefits for the students and also benefits for the teachers participating.*

Graduating teachers are better educated todayMy mind begins to race as I try and anticipate Simone's thinking on quality. I take a bite of the chocolate mud cake I ordered. It tastes good. I smile. "Do you think pre-service teachers were as well prepared as you for teaching?"

Well actually probably better. They seem to have more prac[tical] experience. The education scene is totally different from when I graduated and I am not sure how well I would cope graduating today. I did my pracs [practical experience] in settings that were in many ways similar to the setting I taught in, so I had a fairly good idea of how it was supposed to work. On the flip side I was 20 years old running a kindergarten with a 16 year old untrained teacher aide. I sometimes wonder why those parents felt safe leaving their children with us! A quality kindergarten teacher however is caring, hands-on, kind, able to communicate with children families and able to scaffold children's learning. I ask- Do I want this person teaching my children?

Simone and I laugh and we talk about her rural experience. This leads into a conversation about families.

"How do families perceive a pre-service teacher in their kindergarten?" I ask.

They are heavily influenced by the attitude of the teacher. If the teacher "talks up" the role of the kindergarten in supporting the student as a 'learner' it is usually okay. It also depends on the skills and attitude of the student and how much they express their appreciation to the parents.

"So the teacher is responsible for the bridge between pre-service teacher and parents?"

Pre-service teachers need experience in dealing with families. The only opportunity they have is on professional experience. It is really difficult and not something that is often talked about. This is such an important area of early childhood education.

Personal Gratitude Is Needed from the University

I nod and take a sip of coffee. I am interested to see if Simone could suggest areas of improvement. "So how do you think assessment during professional experience could be improved?"

I think that it should be done as part of a team effort. Teachers (particularly in stand alone settings) feel they have a huge responsibility to ensure that the student is going to be well enough prepared to teach "real children". They are doing this with limited time, and often limited skills for working with adults. I think their role needs to be more carefully looked at. The benefits/ responsibilities also need to be more clearly articulated so that teachers are more likely to take students and feel good about doing so. I don't think the money makes much difference, other incentives are needed. Personal thanks from a university supervisor is very powerful.

"Have you ever got a personal thanks?" I ask quietly. I wonder if the university supervisor's at my current institution manage to say those powerful words.

Rarely have I got a personal thanks.

I feel embarrassed. I have also been a university supervisor and wonder if I forgot to say thank you. I feel ashamed that a person just needed to hear the words 'thanks'. Did the university supervisors really forget the humanness in personal relationships? This person didn't want incentives, just two words that take less than 10 seconds to say. I pause and breathe in slowly. "And what do you think would be useful for pre-service teachers on professional experience?"

I think it works best when students have a long term relationship with the centre and become part of the teaching team, known by children and parents. More time at the centre also makes them more useful because you don't spend half your time telling how they can help. For it all to work there needs to be pay off for everyone in the community -children, preservice teacher, supervising teacher, other staff & parents.

PRE-SERVICE TEACHER STORY

Talia has a previous career in marketing and ran a successful home business before undertaking a graduate diploma of early childhood education. She is in her early 30s and was looking for a career change that will allow her to also spend more time with her children. She has a husband and two children, aged seven and aged two.

Talia wanted to become a teacher to help other children enjoy learning after teaching her own children. She is passionate about helping diverse groups of children. After she had graduated from a Graduate Diploma of Early Childhood Education Talia was offered a job in an independent school. Talia is currently working in a cycle 1 class in a Steiner themed school. She will stay with the children next when they move to year 2. The school

CHAPTER 5

is located within a natural rainforest and is based on developing the social and emotional wellbeing of children. In the morning children engage in meditation, yoga and music before starting literacy activities. She tells me that holistic education lies at the core of the school's philosophy.

I meet her for dinner at a new organic pizza place she has found. We order a spelt pizza and organic ginger beer.

I ask Talia about her time during professional experience.

COMMUNICATION IS IMPORTANT

She takes a sip of ginger beer and smiles. *I had a great professional experience because of a very supportive supervising teacher. We had a great relationship. Our communications were open and honest which allowed me to improve my teaching in class. She told me what I needed to do and I would listen. I would also ask her questions about what I thought about the situation.*

I think one of the enablers was she understood exactly what I had to do for the university. She also responded listened and responded to how I was feeling about the placement. Communication was really important, especially as she was also my assessor of my actions.

I think one of the strange things is that the relationship has to be built in an instant. I can understand why for some students and supervising teachers it wouldn't work because it is such a short time –either four or six weeks to form a relationship and develop an open communication strategy. There is limited time to develop a working relationship. Mine was always a novice expert relationship. It is difficult as well because the supervising teacher doesn't have time to understand the pre-service teachers' background and strengths. In my case it worked well but for some of my friends it didn't. There is sometimes a mismatch between what the supervising teacher expects and the strengths of the pre-service teacher.

I smile at Talia. "So your experience was positive, but how would you have coped if it was negative?"

I think not to panic. I would have taken it as a life learning experience. We always learn from things if they are positive or negative. I would ask myself what could I learn from this negative experience to help me next time.

Assessment Should Be Made by Someone Who Knows the Teaching Profession

I think about what Talia has said. "So what about assessment, how did you find that?"

74

Assessment should be conducted by the supervising teacher because they know the teaching profession best and know what a teacher is to do. There could possibly be a conflict if the teacher and pre-service teacher have not built a solid working relationship for the assessment to take place. I feel the supervising teacher would have the best understanding of any pre-service teachers' abilities and qualities and are best suited to assessing the student. This in effect is what teachers do and act in the classroom. The teacher has seen how I act in the classroom and is capable of making a judgement. I know they have to be a mentor but it is also good they assess. The university's role is to provide an outside third party to mediate any challenges the student and teacher may be facing. They find solutions between the two parties. If there is no challenge, they don't really have a role.

The University Supervisor Didn't Add Value

I take a bite of the freshly arrived pizza. I think of how black and white the situation appears to the former pre-service teacher. "Could you tell me a little about your experiences with your university supervisor?"

To be honest it didn't add much value. There were two visits and I feel that they were of no real benefit. In both practical placements the university teacher I guess had a good instinctive feeling on the students that they were signing off and their respective progress. She came, she signed the correct paper work for the assessment and she left. I think they don't really worry about successful supervisions. They probably have their hands full with problem supervisions. I am not quite sure though what experience the university teacher had in early childhood. She had previously been a primary school teacher so maybe she couldn't comment much about my context.

Improved Handbooks and Forms Are Needed

"So how could the assessment be improved?" I ask.

Talia breathes in slowly. *Well first that handbook for students with assessment is so confusing. It needs to be smaller and more concise. There is so much reading there for students and the supervising teacher. Because the supervising teacher is time poor, they often ask us what we are supposed to be doing. Then all the paperwork and assessments at the end to align with the professional standards is ridiculous. Surely there is a better way to do it. One thing that does worry me though is when my friends and I used to talk, they would say that their teachers would want to show improvement. To do this in the form they would sometimes be*

CHAPTER 5

marked as unsatisfactory in the interim report so the teacher could show improvement of the student's performance by marking satisfactory in the final report. I sometimes wonder though how these judgements are made. How do you ensure that how one supervising teacher marks is the same as the other supervising teacher. At the end of the day I think teachers make a judgement on whether they can see you teaching their current class of children. It is a holistic judgement about whether you should be a teacher or not. There are quite a lot of boxes to tick but I think a teacher makes one judgement.

She pauses. *The other thing that is really difficult is still having university assessment due at the same time and trying to conduct professional experience. I am talking about the theory subject back at university. There should be no assessment due for these subjects during professional experience. The professional experience should be a time when you can fully concentrate on what you are doing and working towards passing the professional experience assessment.*

I ask, "What is a quality early childhood teacher?"

Someone who is able to support children, caring and be competent with the standards for teaching. Teaching in early childhood and primary school are the same as the standards are the same for competency. Quality equals standards.

UNIVERSITY TEACHER STORY

I meet Megan Miles at the university coffee shop. She has been busy preparing her classes for her afternoon teaching. Megan is employed as a sessional academic and has previously been a primary school teacher with over 20 years experience. She teaches into many of the primary school teacher education courses and is completing a PhD. She hopes to move into a full time academic position when she has completed her PhD and there is a position available. I decide not to ask the dreaded question "How is your thesis going?"

I order a coffee for us both and sit down. The sun is warming our backs on the cold day.

I move in the hard chair as I turn the recorder on. I ask Megan to tell me about being a university supervisor to professional experience students.

Well I often have a lot of students to visit. Last semester I had around 22 students which meant a lot of school visits. The students are in a variety of courses. Sometimes I supervise early childhood pre-service teacher students as well as primary pre-service teacher students. I had 40 one semester and

ASSESSMENT IS A HOLISTIC JUDGEMENT

that was really busy for visiting. It really depends on how many students are located in the school as that is how the students are allocated.

I am amazed at how many students Megan supervises. "How do you manage it?"

Well each student is entitled to two visits. To be honest, it is really difficult. Sometimes you have to just try and fit everyone in to a set amount of time. If there is no problem it runs like clock work but if there is a problem, you have to go out more often and try and work out the problem. Sometimes the teacher doesn't like to tell the student there is a problem so that is my job. It has been a little difficult to also supervise the pre-service teachers in the early childhood course. They do things differently to us in primary education. For example planning and documenting learning. I wouldn't accept their lesson planning in my classroom if they were primary school teachers.

It Is Hard to Get Time with the Teacher

I nod at Megan. "So what do you do on a visit?"

Well it is really hard to get time with the teacher. I usually see the student and ask how it is going. I check their folder to see what they have been doing. I then have a quick chat with the teacher. I don't observe the student teaching. That type of feedback comes from the supervising teacher. My role is to check that the handbook is being followed and the student is able to complete areas of their folder to document their professional experience. We then have to make sure that they are working towards the professional standards for teachers.

We Need to Think about What We Are Doing

I am intrigued. "So you never actually observe and provide feedback to the pre-service teacher engaging or teaching the children?"

No there is no time for that. I only have 30 minutes per student. It is also difficult because the student may not be teaching when I come out. If they are you usually take them outside to see how they are going. You then talk to the teacher if she is free however she has to keep supervising the children in the class. By the time I've stayed and observed, checked folders and spoke to everyone it would be over 30 minutes. This is why I think we really need to think about what we are doing in professional experience. It seems like an 'add-on' experience but it is one of the most important in teacher education.

I breathe in slowly. "So what do you think about the assessment of the professional experience?"

CHAPTER 5

Well to be honest I have seen this from both sides- the teacher and the university. I really think there needs to be a stronger type of assessment process for the professional experience. The university knows it has some students who aren't suitable for a school but they have to send them out on professional experience to let them try. It always ends in disaster with more stress for the teacher and school. It is horrible being a supervising teacher and having a student who can't teach and control the class. The poor teacher has to write negative things on the interim report so that I can then intervene. If she doesn't mark the student as unsatisfactory, I can't intervene. The whole process is a little loopy. The teacher has to be an expert, mentor and assessor to the pre-service teacher. You really wouldn't let a doctor who you thought wasn't going to make it loose with patients on their first experience. But we do that in education- we let the pre-service teachers have a go with the children in a real class with a real teacher. If the lesson goes badly, the children have missed out on a quality learning experience. The supervising teacher sometimes has to stand back and give the pre-service teacher a go, even if they know that it is going to be a disaster.

It is really difficult when you have to try and talk to the student about their poor performance. Some are receptive to feedback but other students will just begin to get angry and yell at you. I had one situation where the pre-service teacher wrote a nasty note to the teacher and I had to intervene. It all stemmed from the supervising teacher marking the pre-service teacher as unsatisfactory at the interim report. Trying to get the student to reflect on her behavior was a nightmare. She eventually dropped out but not after a lot of stress to myself and the teacher. How do you tell someone that they are unsatisfactory when they are so certain they are not? I used to sit in that classroom and observe and then talk to the student. She still couldn't see that some of her behaviours were inappropriate. She would yell and started to call people 'dummies'. She would argue that she was a better teacher than all of us – even though she had no experience in the classroom. We had numerous phone calls etc and visits as we had to document everything that was going on. The poor teacher was so turned off by the event she decided never to have a pre-service teacher again.

Assessment Is Like Box Ticking

I am stunned. "Do you think the assessment is fair?"

To be honest, it is a load of box ticking against the standards. The report is really long for time-poor teachers. It probably is a quick way to measure the students against the standards. It doesn't really assess what it should

78

ASSESSMENT IS A HOLISTIC JUDGEMENT

assess in teaching. It has been created to assess what the government thinks is suitable standards for teaching. The other problem I have is that what is considered as satisfactory and unsatisfactory is different to different teachers. They have different understanding and interpretation. For example, some teachers think the pre-service teacher is still developing and will meet the standards one day. Others think that the pre-service teacher should be highly competent right from the beginning. They need to jump in 'head first' and take on most of the duties. The standards mean different things to different people. I even know I differ in my understanding to some of the teachers.

I also have a problem with standards- they limit creativity. While they imply a level to reach, it doesn't encourage people to move beyond the level of competency to become highly competent. We want teachers to share a standard but we also want them to be the best they can. The standards don't do that at all when they are linked to assessment.

So getting back to your question, do I think assessment is fair. I would say no, because it doesn't really assess the qualities of a good teacher. A good teacher can be assessed on a judgment- Do I want this person teaching? Do they have the skills I think are important? I sign the forms but I haven't even seen the student teach. I haven't been able to observe what they are like dealing with children and the supervising teacher. I haven't seen them talking to parents and I have not seen them planning and documenting children's learning.

We Need to Have the Same Goals and Outcomes

I take a minute to think about what Megan has said. I think about construct validity of the standards. "So what should assessment in professional experience look like?"

Well for starters there needs to be greater links between the school and the university to ensure that the pre-service teacher is working towards the same goals and outcomes. For example, many of the things I teach at university are difficult to find in some classrooms such as an inquiry based learning approach. Both parties need to talk and define what each other's role is. They need to also look at how they can support and complement one another. I also think it would be great if I could be more active in the observation of the pre-service teacher. The problem is funding. Money seems to run everything and the budgets seem to be getting tighter and tighter. Some universities in Queensland no longer visit students on professional experience. What does that say about professional experience, the supervising teacher and the school? I think it really shows a lack of respect.

CHAPTER 5

Megan takes a big long breath. *Well what really needs to happen is more observation of student teaching. In today's world that could be looking at video cameras in the classroom etc that both the university supervisor and the school supervisor could comment on. That is how you build strong efficacy and agency. We need to allow personalized learning for these future teachers and provide them with constructive feedback to hone their skills. Do you remember when we use to have the glass behind some classrooms? It was fantastic for observing others but also for talking about what the teacher was doing in the classroom. Teaching is very much about experience and reacting in the moment. It is difficult for the current assessment to cover that with really general statements about professional conduct. There needs to be a clear understanding between all parties about what skills and capabilities the pre-service teacher needs to develop and demonstrate to enable them to become a teacher of high quality. If the skills are not demonstrated, they shouldn't be allowed to pass.*

The sun has now moved and the shade starts to creep over. A student approaches Megan for a quick question about an assignment. I smile and wait before continuing the interview.

Would We Really Trust this Person with Children?

"So what does a quality early childhood teacher look like?"

Megan shares a smile.

I use my intuition. It is a judgement call we used to use in school all the time. You ask yourself 'one day they will be teaching my grandchildren Is this what I want?' This is the test I use. I know others who ask the same question. Would we really trust these people with children and their learning? A quality early childhood teacher would pass the test.

I Remember That Was a Good Student

Do you remember a supervision at the kindergarten in 2010 with a student called Talia Brown?

I vaguely remember. It is really sad I don't remember all of it because I have to visit so many different schools, teachers and students. I also have to remember all my students in class.

I show Megan a photo of the kindergarten to remind her, to see if it prompts her memory.

Yes I think I remember. The kindergartens all look the same after a while. It was a female student who was doing well on her professional experience-

80

no problems at all so that is probably why I can't remember much about it. I would have just signed off on her reports and folders. She was working well with the teacher and the teacher was really supportive. I think I was there for about 30 minutes. It was difficult to talk to the teacher, as it always is because the teacher has to keep teaching and supervising the teaching. I always have a quick chat to the teacher if I can. I sometimes wonder if they feel like I am just checking up. It creates an awful power imbalance. Rather than working together to help the assessment of the student, I become the assessor of the assessor. I can understand why some teachers have given up taking pre-service teachers. There is just too much work with assessment and then they think I am assessing what they assessed. It is strange because when we chat to the teacher, we never talk about the actual content in the assessment. It is kept pretty general – How is the student going? Anything I should know? Any problems? Those types of questions. The more I talk this through with you the more problems I am seeing with professional experience and the assessment of professional experience.

Megan pauses.

It is actually pretty sad that I don't remember the successful students. They are doing an amazing job on their professional experience and I can't spend more time with them to see ways to enhance their practice. My time is really taken up with trying to deal with the problem professional experiences. I feel really bad that I didn't spend more time with this student. Is she ok now?

I smile at Megan. "Yes she is working in Brisbane. She was employed straight after graduation".

I like to hear those happy endings. We all need happy endings to show that what we are doing, as crazy and as time poor as we are, does have some successes.

****

CHAPTER 6

THE FUTURE AND NARRATIVE CONSTELLATIONS

INTRODUCTION

After reading the examples of the narrative constellations in the past chapters, you will have hopefully a better understanding of a narrative constellation. All of the examples presented are intended to highlight the lived experience of the participants. The final chapter brings together all that we know about narrative constellations and provides possible suggestions for future research. It is only by looking at the past that we are able to suggest possibilities for the future.

The process of narration is also a culture-specific process that can represent a potential framework for enhancing contextualist theories of development (Bruner, 1990; Singer, 2004). Narrative can bridge cultural modes of thinking and the ways in which participants come to reasons and behave in culture-specific ways. In this way, participant's thinking reflects the modes of thinking of those who collectively make up a particular cultural group in which the participants collaborate. Contemporary issues of place become important in analysis. The concept of place becomes a key features in how participants interact and communicate with each other.

As you read the final section, you are also encouraged to think about the potential of narrative constellations for your own lived experience. What could be revealed from undertaking a narrative constellation on yourself? Would there be some alternate perspectives that you did not think about? Perhaps narrative constellation provides you with another version of reality to understand the nature of the world.

WHAT HAVE WE LEARNT FROM NARRATIVE CONSTELLATIONS?

When we look at narrative constellations we can learn many things about phenomena, participants and also ourselves as researchers. The importance is to be open to such research that explores concepts of lived experience. By being open we can allow ourselves to also provide new understandings about

CHAPTER 6

the world around us. One potential area where narrative constellations have been used is education.

Some functions well served by narratives are "to share experiences, the presentation of self (identity work), create continuity in learning through connecting the child's home with their preschool, collective remembering and learning to attend and to what, for example the educator or, by extension, the community, considers to be essential" (Pramling & Odegaard, 2011, p. 30). Research has also found that children who may not be the storyteller can also learn narrative skills by being present, listening and becoming familiar with narrative genre. (Rogoff et al., 2003). This means everyday activities that involve collective groups constitute important spaces for gradually learning to narrate.

Narrative is considered a key concept in considering communicative development in the child (Kamberelis, 1999). In many early childhood settings for children aged birth to 5 years, appropriating the paradigmatic of reasoning is already recognised in many activities such as categorization games and informational, expository texts (such as picture books about natural sciences) (Mantzicopoulos & Patrick, 2010). Greater awareness and understanding however is needed for the widespread importance of narrative as a sense-making form for young children in early childhood settings (Bamberg, 2007; Bruner, 1990, 2002; Kamberelis, 1999; Ochs and Capps, 1996; 2001; Tomasello, 1999; van Oers, 2003). The role of an early years educator is to scaffold young children's narrative skills, allowing them to tell a story in an interesting and intelligible way (Odegaard, 2007).

When a child tells a story (even as a word or a sentence) they not only want to tell the story, they want to tell it to someone (Pramling & Odegaard, 2011). Utterances are given meaning in human interaction in the way others respond to them (Bakhtin, 1986). The role of the educator is therefore not only to develop the narrative skills of the child, but also to be interested and communicate that they are interested in the emerging narrative. Through questions, the educator will be able to direct young children's attention towards what they consider worth telling (Aukrust, 1996; Odegaard, 2006).

Narrative constellations provide opportunities to bridge the gap between the home and school environments. Narrative constellations are able to achieve this in a number of ways. Narratives provide a starting point for educators to understand children's currents funds of knowledge for technology and arts from their home environments. This includes interactions with children to engage an understanding of what their current practices are with technology and the arts. This can also be aided by regular communication with families

84

THE FUTURE AND NARRATIVE CONSTELLATIONS

about the involvement of technology and arts in the child's life. Families may want to share experiences of what types of activities children regularly engage in.

Many stories are shared by children in early childhood and school settings. Stories in classrooms are more scripted than home environments as educators engage with large groups of children at once (Dickinson, 1991). When a child is at home that may have informal and less structured conversations with adults with one or a few children. Narratives in school are shared in a different environment and context. At school, the structure of the classroom dictates the types of narratives that are shared in the preschool and the characteristics of the story. Narratives in schools are generally shorter than those shared at home (Dickenson, 1991), however they are also more diverse in form and expose children to a variety of interactions with other children that may not be experienced at home (Dickenson, 2001). Children experience different topics and different narrative structures.

Narrative can also allow daily interactions between educators and children to construct knowledge together about arts and technology. Young children's social interaction with their friends and educators encourage their knowledge construction in developmentally appropriate ways (Colker, 2011). Meaningful social interaction can be explained by the Zone of Proixmal Development (Vygotsky, 1978). The Zone of Proximal Development is the area of development a child has not reached on his own, but can reach with the assistance from others. According to Vygotsky, 'every function in a child's cultural development appears twice, first on the social level (interpsychological), and later on the individual level (intrapsychological) (Vygotsky, 1978, p.57). Examples of cultural development appearing twice could include narratives during informal situations such as meal time or formal situations such as circle time in the morning or a focused teaching segment.

From a teachers perspective can also highlight the complexity of relationships between teachers working together, principals, community and with parents. Teachers and principals are also asked to reflect on their own personal and professional identity in order to reflect on the complexity of lived experience. We are also able to see the complex relationship within each of the paired stories that operate with and against each other. It is these tensions between the paired stories that also only become known by engaging with a story constellation approach. We begin to see the importance of understanding the lived experience of the individual.

Research is beginning to really focus on the concept of lived experience, not only in education but also in other disciplines. This especially includes

CHAPTER 6

health and wellbeing. Within disciplines there is a refocus on the importance of understanding the self and the beliefs associated with personal experiences. For example in education, how teachers feel and experience the world informs how they teach. In medicine, it is important to know the lived experience of patients who experience illness, as well as medical professionals who treat ilness.

The focus on lived experience also seeks to unify the body with the mind. As the research community grows in understanding physical representations of phenomena, there is also a need to focus on the mind and the concept of living and experiencing the phenomena.

One theory useful for adults to understand in considering narrative constellations and future research is interaction theory. Interaction theory is described as a larger enactive or phenomenological approach to social cognition (Gallagher, 2012). Interaction theory (Gallagher, 2013, p.5) relies "on developmental studies that demonstrate that our encounters with others are best characterized in terms of embodied interactions rather than the kind of mindreading defended by simulation theory or other theory-of-mind approaches".

While it is important to realize the potential of narratives for participants, we must also visit the limitations and challenges when interpreting narratives in terms of participant experiences. Although researchers may be offered insight into participant lives, there is a need for researchers not to simplify the interpretation of these stories. For example, as an adult, we must acknowledge that while we can prompt and be involved in children's narrations, we do not have unfettered access to children's experiences. We also can not generalize children or adults. From participant narrative constellations, it is therefore difficult to provide international comparison or a generalized conclusion.

Another limitation is that in accordance with narrative scholars, it is also acknowledged that researchers and educators do not have direct access to human experience. Rather it is only a participant's reported experience. The inaccessibility is more evident with pre-verbal children who are unable to report their experiences. However, some contemporary research on children's experiences also emphasises the symbolic as well as socially mediated and shared nature of experience (Greene & Hill, 2006).

WHAT ABOUT THE FUTURE?

The possibilities with narrative constellations are endless. It is important to remember that when we explore research surrounding humans, we can also consider the lived experience of the phenomena. This means that the potential

THE FUTURE AND NARRATIVE CONSTELLATIONS

of narrative constellations can be extended to any discipline, including health, pyschology, education, sociology, anthropology and many more. We know that when we involve participants in sharing their lived experiences, we are opening new worlds into their experiences and beliefs.

Researchers are urged to consider the importance of narrative constellations for thier own research agendas. By exploring the concepts of lived experience we begin in our research to unite the mind and body. We may also come to realise the importance of cultural understanding of phenomena and what this means for each individual. Rather than be a one off, narrative constellations have the potential to be benefical for anyone who is involved in research with humans.

Policy makers may also find narrative constellations useful for governmental policy. Insights into gaps between official policy and what the lived experience is for individuals provides an important insight into the success and failures of policy. As countries move to improve the implementation of policy, it is important for research to consider and report the influence on personal experience. The gap between policy and lived experience therefore becomes an important area of negotiation.

Narrative constellations are respectful of the research participant. This is perhaps a turning point in research ideas and provides a better balance of power between the researcher and participant. In narrative constellations everything can be negotiated with the participant. Even the concept of participant can be challenged with some engaged in narrative constellations using the terminology of co-researcher. Nevertheless, narrative constellations provide important reflections about power relations in the research process and allows us to consider the researcher and participants role in the creation and presentation of data.

Narrative constellations also have the potential to be used alongside quanitative research (such as surveys) in a mixed methods approach. Such research then provides impotant information about the breadth and depth of the phenomena under study. While researchers may have a theoretical understanding such as a reported statistic, narrative constellations can be used to describe exactly what the statistics means for individuals living the phenomena. In essence, the narrative constellation will describe and provide a deeper understanding of human existence within the research problem.

The future is endless with the use of narrative constellations. In contemporary times we must embrace and understand the importance of culture and the influence of culture on lived experience. This means accepting that each culture is different and may provide a different lived

CHAPTER 6

experience for the participant. Variation can occur for many factors and provide investigators with a deeper understanding of the importance of contextual and cultural factors.

Finally, narrative constellations also allow researchers to reflect on their own positions and biases. It is hoped that through such practice, researchers are able to improve their own practice and realise the importance of their actions and thoughts. As researchers it is important to engage in reflective practice to see how our own experiences shape the way we research. Our influence as humans becomes known and reflected upon. By building better practices, we can design and carete better research.

CONCLUSION

This book was written to show the importance of narrative constellations as an emerging research method. The new approach allows new understanding of human perspectives and experiences and provides greater insights into the participant's worlds and meaning-making. While they achieve greater empowerment for participants, it is important however to consider that methods and techniques with participants still needs to be reflexively and critically approached.

In the book I have shown the importance of narrative constellations. The intention is to highlight a variety of ways narrative can be used as an analytical tool by researchers and others working with lived experience. I believe narratives are an important contemporary approach for understanding humans and their understanding of the world. I also believe that narratives provide important insights into the cultural contexts in which people live. It is hoped that after reading this text, you are able to see the importance of narrative constellation research and consider engaging with narrative practice.

My journey with narrative constellations began with my PhD studies and have grown and continued until today. Everytime I encage with narrative constellations I learn more about the importance of listening and hearing lived experience. I also become more aware of the complex nature of life, experiences and cultural surroundings. I am honoured to have found narrative constellations and been able to build upon and work with this important research methodology. I hope that others can find similar journeys and beginnings with narrative constellations. I wish you well on your journey!

THE FUTURE AND NARRATIVE CONSTELLATIONS

REFERENCES

Aukrust, V. G. (1996). Learning to talk and keep silent about everyday routines: A study of verbal interaction between young children and their caregivers. *Scandinavian Journal of Educational Research, 40*(4), 311–324.

Bakhtin, M. M. (1986). The problem of speech genres. In C. Emerson & M. Holquist (Eds.), *Speech genres and other late essays* (V. W. McGee, Trans., pp. 60–102). Austin, TX: University of Texas Press.

Bamberg, M. G. W. (Ed.). (2007). *Narrative: State of the art*. Amsterdam, The Netherlands: John Benjamins.

Bruner, J. S. (1990). *Acts of meaning*. Cambridge, MA: Harvard University Press.

Bruner, J. S. (2002). *Making stories: Law, literature, life*. Cambridge, MA: Harvard University Press.

Colker, L. J. (2011). Technology and learning: What early childhood educators have to say. *Teaching Young Children, 4*(3), 25–27.

Dickinson, D. K. (1991). Teacher agenda and setting: Constraints on conversation in preschools. In A. McCabe & C. Peterson (Eds.), *Developing narrative structure* (pp. 255–301). Hillsdale, NJ: Erlbaum.

Dickinson, D. K., & Tabors, P. O. (Eds.). (2001). *Beginning literacy with language: Young children learning at home and in school*. Baltimore, MD: Brookes.

Gallagher, S. (2012). In defense of phenomenological approaches to social cognition: Interacting with the critics. *Review of Philosophy and Psychology, 3*, 187–212.

Gallagher, S. (2013). An education in narratives. *Educational Philosophy and Theory*, 1–10.

Greene, S., & Hill, M. (2006). Researching children's experience: Methods and methodological issues. In S. Greene & D. Hogan (Eds.), *Researching children's experience: Approaches and methods* (pp. 1–21). London, UK: Sage.

Kamberelis, G. (1999). Genre development and learning: Children writing stories, science reports, and poems. *Research in the Teaching of English, 33*(4), 403–460.

Mantzicopoulos, P., & Patrick, H. (2010). The seesaw is a machine that goes up and down: Young children's narrative responses to science-related informational text. *Early Education and Development, 21*(3), 412–444.

Ochs, E., & Capps, L. (1996). Narrating the self. *Annual Review of Anthropology, 25*, 19–43.

Ochs, E., & Capps, L. (2001). *Living narrative: Creating lives in everyday storytelling*. Cambridge, MA: Harvard University Press.

Ødegaard, E. E. (2006). What's worth talking about? Meaning-making in toddler-initiated conarratives in preschool. *Early Years, 26*(1), 79–92.

Ødegaard, E. E. (2007). Meningsskaping i barnehagen: Innehold og bruk av barns og voksnes samtalefortellinger [Meaning making in preschool: Contents and use of children's and adults' co-narratives]. *Göteborg Studies in Educational Sciences, 255*. Göteborg, Sweden: Acta Universitatis Gothoburgensis.

Pramling, N., & Ødegaard, E. E. (2011). Learning to narrate: Appropriating a cultural mould for sense-making and communication. In N. Pramling & I. Pramling Samuelsson (Eds.), *Educational encounters: Nordic studies in early childhood didactics* (pp. 15–35). Dordrecht, The Netherlands: Springer.

Rogoff, B., Paradise, R., Mejía Arauz, R., Correa-Cháves, M., & Angelillo, C. (2003). Firsthand learning through intent participation. *Annual Review of Psychology, 54*, 175–203.

CHAPTER 6

Singer, J. A. (2004). Narrative identity and meaning making across the adult lifespan: An introduction. *Journal of Personality, 72*, 437–459.

Tomasello, M. (1999). *The cultural origins of human cognition.* Cambridge, MA: Harvard University Press.

van Oers, B. (Ed.). (2003). *Narratives of childhood: Theoretical and practical explorations for the innovation of early childhood education.* Amsterdam, The Netherlands: VU University Press.

Vygotsky, L. (1978). *Mind in society: The development of higher psychological processes.* Cambridge, MA: Harvard University Press.